THE HISTORY OF
BRITAIN
COMPANION

Jo Swinnerton

A THINK BOOK FOR

ROBSON
BOOKS

The Birdwatcher's Companion
by Malcolm Tait and Olive Tayler

The Cook's Companion
by Jo Swinnerton

The Countryside Companion
by Malcolm Tait and Olive Tayler

The Fishing Companion
by Lesley Crawford

The Gardener's Companion
by Vicky Bamforth

The Golfer's Companion
by Chris Martin

The History of Britain Companion
by Jo Swinnerton

The Ideas Companion
by Johnny Acton

The Legal Companion
by Vincent Powell

The Literary Companion
by Emma Jones

The London Companion
by Jo Swinnerton

The Moviegoer's Companion
by Rhiannon Guy

The Politics Companion
Edited by Daisy Sampson

The Sailing Companion
by Miles Kendall

The Shakespeare Companion
by Emma Jones and Rhiannon Guy

The Traveller's Companion
by Georgina Newbery and Rhiannon Guy

The Walker's Companion
by Malcolm Tait

The Wildlife Companion
by Malcolm Tait and Olive Tayler

SERIES EDITORS

Malcolm Tait, Emma Jones, Jo Swinnerton and Rhiannon Guy

I warmly welcome your eager desire to know something of the doings and sayings of the great men of the past, and of our own nation, in particular.

The Venerable Bede

THINK
A Think Book
for Robson Books

First published in United Kingdom in 2005 by
Robson Books
151 Freston Road, London W10 6TH

An Imprint of Anova Books Company Ltd

Edited by Jo Swinnerton
Companion team: Tilly Boulter, James Collins, Rhiannon Guy,
Emma Jones, Lou Millward Tait, Matt Packer, Sonja Patel,
and Malcolm Tait

Think Publishing
The Pall Mall Deposit
124–128 Barlby Road, London W10 6BL
www.thinkpublishing.co.uk

ISBN 9781861059147

10 9 8 7 6 5 4 3 2

Printed and bound by MPG Books Ltd, Bodmin, Cornwall

www.anovabooks.com

There is always something rather absurd about the past.

Max Beerbohm

WITH THANKS AND TOP MARKS IN THEIR HISTORY TESTS...

To my father, Iain, and brother, Alastair, for their invaluable contributions to this book; and to Godfrey for his constant supply of ideas, encouragement and pheasant soup.

INTRODUCTION

It can be surprisingly useful to know that England's longest parliament lasted 17 years, that the first British speeding ticket was issued to a motorist doing eight miles per hour, and that a Welshman named Captain Mainwaring invented lawn tennis. And you may one day be glad to know that five and half yards used to be called a pole, that there were 38 vineyards in England in 1086 and that tenth-century physicians cured baldness with burned bees.

For history is not just about kings, queens and battles (although much of it is, and they are in here too). It is also about the smaller things – the inventor of the bicycle, the first woman to parachute from a hot-air balloon and the possible identity of Robin Hood. It is these intriguing facts that fill all the holes in the rich fabric of our history.

So within these pages you will indeed find the Wars of the Roses, the wives of Henry VIII and the Battle of Culloden, as is right and proper. But you will also find out why Dr Crippen's head fell off, why William Cobbett hated potatoes and why 3 September 1752 never existed. And you will be reminded, once more, of the many and varied pleasures to be found in Britain's marvellous history.

Jo Swinnerton, Editor

DAMP SQUIBS

In 1749, the Peace of Aix-la-Chapelle was celebrated with a huge fireworks display in Green Park in London. Handel composed his Music for the Royal Fireworks especially for it and rehearsals went well. But sadly the warning that a good rehearsal means a bad performance came true. The fireworks were ruined by heavy rain, although not before they had set fire to the pavilion by going off prematurely, and the evening ended with a large public brawl.

KNOW YOUR RIGHTS

Acts that limited the power of the monarch

Charter of Liberties	1100	Henry I
Magna Carta	1215	John
Provisions of Oxford	1258	Henry III
Confirmatio Cartarum	1297	Edward I
Lords Ordainers appointed	1310	Edward II
Petition of Right	1628	Charles I
Habeas Corpus	1679	Charles II
Bill of Rights	1689	William III and Mary
First Mutiny Bill	1689	William III and Mary
Act of Settlement	1701	William III

THE OLDEST CLOCK IN THE WORLD

The oldest surviving working clock in the world can be found in Salisbury Cathedral in Wiltshire. Dating from 1386, it has no face, but strikes the hours to indicate the time. It was replaced in 1884 by a new clock and languished in the tower until 1929, when it was rediscovered and put on display. It was restored to its original condition in 1956. It is estimated to have ticked more than five million times.

GREAT BRITISH FIRSTS

The first glider in the world capable of carrying a passenger was designed by Sir George Cayley in 1853. It consisted of a kite-shaped wing with a surface area of 500 square feet, and a tricycle undercarriage for the pilot. Instead of making the maiden flight himself, however, Sir George persuaded his coachman to do it for him. The coachman bravely covered about 500 yards before coming to earth with a crash, and was heard to cry out 'Please, Sir George, I wish to give notice, I was hired to drive, not to fly!' Nevertheless, he earned his place in history as the pilot of the first true aeroplane flight.

THE KNIGHTS OF THE GARTER

In the reign of King Edward III, the King resolved to gather around him the best soldiers of Europe, in the manner of King Arthur's knights, and announced that a jousting tournament would be held on 19 January 1345, at which the knights would be selected. Edward had St George's Chapel built at Windsor and commissioned a 200-foot round table at which to seat the knights. He devised a costume bearing the image of St George tilting at a dragon, and a piece of blue ribbon that they should always wear around their necks. After the Battle of Crecy in 1346, he formalised this collection of knights as the Most Noble Order of the Garter, to which the Knights of the Garter belonged. He proclaimed that he would choose 25 of the bravest knights, and would himself be the twenty-sixth member of the order. Their motto was 'Honi soit qui mal y pense' (shame be his who thinks ill of it), supposedly the words of Edward as he tied to his leg a blue garter dropped by a lady at court. The words are written on the blue garter worn by all the knights on their left leg. Twenty-five knights are still appointed by the sovereign, and since 1987 women have also been eligible.

QUOTE UNQUOTE

Gladstone in Great Britain and Parnell in Ireland, under the watchword, 'Home Rule for Ireland', are fighting the battle of self-government for all mankind.
Rutherford Birchard Hayes, US president

HISTORIC WORDS

A large Whale taken, twixt my Land butting on the Thames and Greenwich, which drew an infinite Concourse to see it, by water, horse, coach, on foote from Lond, and all parts. It appeared first below Greenewich at low-water, for at high water, it would have destroyed all the boates: but lying now in shallow water, incompassed with boates, after a long Conflict it was killed with the harping yrons, and struck in the head, out of which spouted blood and water, by two tunnels like Smoake, from a chimney: and after an horrid grone it ran quite on shore and died. The length was 58 foote: 16in heights, black skin'd like Coach-leather, very small eyes, greate taile, small finns and but 2: a piked snout, a mouth so wide and divers men might have stood upright in it: No teeth at all but sucked the slime onely as thro a grate made of that bone which we call Whale bone: The throate [yet] so narrow, as would not have admitted the least of fishes.
From the diary of John Evelyn, 3 June 1658

While Alfred was very proud of his newfangled plane, his wife was less than happy with the inflight facilities.

WHO WAS LORD HAW-HAW?

Just before the outbreak of World War Two, American-born William Joyce slipped out of England, where he had been studying at the London School of Economics, and headed for Germany. He had been a vociferous supporter of Oswald Mosley's fascist union, but felt so unappreciated by Mosley that he set up his own pro-Nazi organisation, called the National Socialist League. From his new home, he then made regular propaganda broadcasts in English, beginning each speech with the phrase 'Germany calling'. He developed an exaggerated public-school accent to hide his own Cockney/Irish tones and no doubt to further infuriate his listeners, which gave rise to the nickname 'Lord Haw-Haw'. Treated with derision by the English, he was tried for treason and executed after the war, as he held a British, rather than an American, passport.

In 1705, British astronomer Edmund Halley predicted that the comet seen in 1531, 1607 and 1682 would return in 1758. When it did indeed return as predicted, it was named in his honour, although Halley didn't live to see it. His calculation that it appeared every 76 years or thereabouts enabled historians to show that the comet has been recorded in literature, art and even stone tablets all the way back to 240BC. Many of its appearances have been taken as portents or omens, and it has shown up at some big moments in history. For instance:

January 66AD – The comet hovered over Jerusalem, prompting Jewish historian Josephus to write that it heralded the destruction of the city. Of course it could be argued that his 'prophesy' helped start the Jewish Revolt of that year, which did indeed lead to the destruction of the city.

June 451 – Attila the Hun's previously invincible forces were finally beaten at the battle of Chalons by an unholy alliance of Imperial Roman and Barbarian troops. But historically it was a Pyrrhic victory. For although Attila died only two years later, the Emperor Romulus was deposed by the Barbarians in 476, effectively ending the western Roman Empire.

October 684 – The comet's appearance in the UK was followed by three months of rain, crop failure and an outbreak of plague. In other words, a typical British winter.

March 1066 – The comet appeared to Duke William of Normandy and King Harold of England. William believed it to be a good sign, and prompt-ly invaded, defeated Harold and became King of England. For the unfortunate Harold, the comet was a very bad sign indeed.

June 1456 – At this point in history, the Turks were on the verge of destroying the entire Christian world. They held Constantinople, and the comet appeared just as they laid siege to Belgrade. At the time it was claimed that Pope Callistus III had excommunicated the comet, and although this is thought to be untrue, whatever he did worked – the Turks were put to flight.

20 April 1910 – The comet coincided with the death of King Edward VII. An astronomer at the time reported that the Earth would pass through the comet's tail, which contained a poisonous gas. The fact that the amounts were so minuscule as to be completely harmless didn't stop many entrepreneurs from making a small fortune selling 'comet pills' which were guaranteed to protect people from harm. It should be noted that he people who took them did, indeed, survive unscathed. As did everyone else.

WHAT DID THEY DO IN THE WAR?

Kingsley Amis	Officer in Royal Corps of Signals
Tony Benn	Fought against Japan in the RAF
Dirk Bogarde	Captain in the Queen's Royal Regiment; helped to liberate Belsen
Roald Dahl	Fighter pilot and wing commander in RAF
Denholm Elliott	RAF, shot down and sent to POW camp
Dick Francis	Officer in the RAF
Denis Healey	Beachmaster at the Anzio landings in Italy
Patrick Macnee	Lieutenant in the Royal Navy
Patrick Moore	Navigator in the RAF with Bomber Command
Jon Pertwee	Royal Navy; on leave from his duties when his ship was sunk by the *Bismarck*
Donald Pleasance	RAF, shot down in France, held in POW camp
Ronald Searle	Captured by Japanese in 1942, worked on Burma-Siam railway
Peter Sellers	Corporal in RAF

KING BEHAVING BADLY

In 955, officials were puzzled when the young King Edwy didn't turn up to his own coronation feast. Puzzlement turned to outrage when the 14-year-old king was discovered in his bedchamber, enjoying the company of a young lady and her mother, his new crown discarded on the floor along with the rest of his clothes.

HISTORIC WORDS

You wretches, detestable on land and sea; you who seek equality with lords are unworthy to live. Give this message to your colleagues. Rustics you were and rustics you are still: you will remain in bondage not as before but incomparably harsher. For as long as we live we will strive to suppress you, and your misery will be an example in the eyes of posterity. However, we will spare your lives if you remain faithful. Choose now which course you want to follow.

The words of 14-year-old King Richard II, as he addressed the Peasants' Revolt of 1381

A few days beforehand, Richard had appeared to sympathise with the peasants' cause and to agree to an end to serfdom. But as the rebels continued to resist, the King lost patience. He rode to where they were assembled and issued his ultimatum, at which many of the peasants gave in and accepted his mercy. The rest were routed by royal troops and the ringleaders were beheaded.

BRITISH RECORD-BREAKERS

In September 2000, the village of Denby Dale, West Yorkshire, upheld a long tradition of marking important national occasions by baking an immense meat pie. The pie weighed 12 tonnes, measured 40 feet long, nine feet wide by three feet deep, and was declared the biggest meat and potato pie in the world.

The Millennium Pie – baked to celebrate the year 2000 and the Queen Mother's 100th birthday – was the tenth in a long series of over-sized Denby Dale pies. The first was baked in 1788 to celebrate the restored health of King George III, and the next to celebrate the Battle of Waterloo. The third marked the repeal of the Corn Laws and the fourth was baked to mark Queen Victoria's Jubilee in 1887. Unfortunately it was discovered that the meat was a bit off and it couldn't be eaten, so the villagers buried the offending pie in a wood and made another one. More recently a pie was baked in 1964 to celebrate four royal births in one year (to the Queen, Princess Margaret, Princess Alexandra and the Duchess of Kent).

At the ceremony for the Millennium Pie, 70-year-old former Coldstream Guard Raymond Haigh was made the Guardian of the Pie, which put him in charge of security and gave him first taste. He reported that it tasted 'beautiful'.

QUOTE UNQUOTE

God spare me long enough to take revenge on you.
What Henry II really said, as he appeared to embrace his
rebellious son Richard in a kiss of peace

ROYAL NICKNAMES

Name	Nickname	So named because...
Edward	Edward the Confessor	Pious; built Westminster Abbey
William I	William the Bastard	Illegitimate
	William the Conqueror	Beat Harold II at the Battle of Hastings
William II	Rufus	Red-faced
Richard I	Richard the Lionheart	Courageous in battle
John	Softsword	Lacked military prowess
John	Lackland	Lacking in land, on account of being the fourth son
Edward I	Longshanks	Very tall
Mary I	Bloody Mary	Executed many Protestants
Elizabeth I	The Virgin Queen	Never married

IT'S JUST A PHASE

Fads we have endured – some of which have come back to haunt us (and some of which never went away):

Tupperware	1945
Bikinis	1946
Polyester	1953
TV dinners	1954
Hula hoops	1958
Barbie dolls	1959
Lava lamps	1964
Waterbeds	1969
Smiley logo	1960s
Bellbottoms	1960s
Mini skirts	1960s
Pet rocks	1970s
Platform shoes	1970s
Flares	1970s
Skateboards	1970s
Pong (first computer game)	1972
Star Wars	1977
Rubik's Cube	1979
Digital watches	1980s
Legwarmers	1980s
Pacman	1980s
Shell suits	1980s
Beanie babies	1990s
Tamagotchi	1997

PAST PUZZLES

What did King John manage to hang on to in 1204?
Answer on page 153.

PAYMENT IN KIND

Early in the eleventh century, the King of Lombardy imposed a tax that would allow English merchants the right to trade tax-free in Pavia, Italy. It was payable once every three years, and consisted of:

- 50lbs of pure silver
- Two greyhounds with gilded collars
- Two shields
- Two swords
- Two lances

The official who collected the tax also had to be paid, and his fee was two fur coats and 2lbs of silver.

GREAT BRITISH FIRSTS:
SCIENTIFIC DISCOVERIES

Who	*Discovered what*
Frederick Banting	Insulin (discovered with CH Best)
James Bradley	Provided evidence that the earth revolved around the sun
Francis Crick	DNA structure (discovered with James Watson)
John Dalton	Atomic theory of matter
Charles Darwin	Theory of evolution and natural selection
Michael Faraday	Electromagnetic induction
Alexander Fleming	Penicillin
William Gilbert	First person to explain magnetism
William Harvey	Circulation of the blood
Joseph Lister	Antisepsis
(Joseph) Norman Lockyer	Existence of helium
Isaac Newton	Gravity
James Simpson	Anaesthetic properties of chloroform

IT WAS ONLY A JOKE

When the radio broadcast of HG Wells's *War of the Worlds* caused widespread panic in the US in 1938, because the listeners took the story of alien invasions a little too seriously, the broadcasters should not have been surprised. The BBC had achieved the same feat only 12 years before. On 16 January 1926, a piece of satire entitled *Broadcasting from the Barricades,* went out on the airwaves, prefaced with the explanation that it was a work of fiction. It then announced that a band of unemployed and angry men had run riot in London, incited to violence and vandalism by the likes of Mr Popplebury, the Secretary of the National Movement for Abolishing Theatre Queues. Big Ben had been destroyed; the National Gallery was besieged; the Savoy Hotel had been blown up; and civil servants were being roasted alive in Trafalgar Square and hung from lampposts. For those listeners who had missed the warning at the beginning, the programme was all too real. The BBC – and the Savoy – were flooded with alarmed phone calls and the BBC was forced to apologise, although it did so with bad grace, promising that in future it would 'take no risks with its public's average standard intelligence'. It also pointed out, somewhat crossly, that had the nation truly been at risk, it would hardly have interspersed the reports of rioting with short bursts of dance music.

MADE IN BRITAIN

When	Who	Invented what
1250	Roger Bacon	Magnifying glass
1596	John Harington	Water closet; it had a flushing cistern that drained into a pit below the house
1614	John Napier	Logarithms
1622	William Oughtred	Slide rule
1680	George Dalgano	Sign-language alphabet
1665	Robert Hooke	Prototype for light microscope
1666	Isaac Newton	Calculus
1668	Isaac Newton	Reflecting telescope
1698	Thomas Savery	Patented first steam engine, which was used to pump water

A CONVENIENT TALE

Thomas Crapper was born in Yorkshire in 1837 and demonstrated his future work ethic by walking to London in 1848, aged 11, in search of a job. He found employment with a plumber in Chelsea, earning four shillings a week. In 1861 he set up on his own under the name of 'The Marlboro' Works of Thomas Crapper and Co'. It was a good time to be a plumber; London had just acquired its first two main sewers, which were to become 83 miles of sewers over the next four years. However, the toilets of London were still primitive structures, and Crapper set out to improve them by inventing the Water Waste Preventer, a flushing cistern that used a minimum of water to flush, had sufficient force to clean the bowl, and refilled itself effortlessly. Having perfected his invention, Crapper exhibited it at the Health Show in 1884. He proved its worth by flushing through a large quantity of 'waste', which comprised 10 apples, one sponge, some pieces of newspaper and some plumber's 'smudge' coated over the toilet pan. He went on to become sanitary engineer to royalty, receiving four royal warrants and installing the drains and bathrooms at the royal residence in Sandringham as well as in Westminster Abbey. Having found his metier, Crapper went on to design cantilevered toilets, automatically flushing cisterns and self-rising closet seats. He also designed a luxury toilet for Lily Langtry, mistress of Edward, Prince of Wales, in the form of an armchair upholstered in velvet, at a cost of £9 12s 6d. He named his toilets after London street names, which included Marlborough, Walton, Cadogan and Sloane. He died in 1910, aged 73, having left an indelible stamp on the history of the city and its cisterns.

**Gluttons whose exploits were so astonishing that
they were recorded in print**

John Marriott, a lawyer during the reign of James I, was the subject of a pamphlet entitled *The Great Eater of Graye's Inn*, or the *Life of Mr Marriott, the Cormorant*, in which he was said to have eaten a lunch prepared for 20 men.

Walter Willey was a brewer's servant celebrated for his gluttony, as proven by the November 1675 edition of the *Annual Register*, which claimed that at one meal Willey devoured a 6lb roast goose, 4lbs of bread and three quarts of porter.

Nicholas Wood was a glutton of such excess that an entire book was devoted to his vice, entitled *The Great Eater of Kent*, or *Part of the Admirable Teeth and Stomach Exploits of Nicholas Wood*. At one meal Wood ate an entire sheep, leaving only the wool, skin, horns and bones, and on occasion he was known to eat 18lbs of black pudding for breakfast.

QUOTE UNQUOTE

Unlike the male codfish which, suddenly finding itself the parent of three million five hundred thousand little codfish cheerfully resolves to love them all, the British aristocracy is apt to look with a somewhat jaundiced eye on its younger sons.
PG Wodehouse, author

WITCHES, PROPHETS AND MYSTIC MEN

Michael Scott was a medieval Scottish intellectual with abilities so exceptional that he was hired to tutor the Holy Roman Emperor Frederick II, and to translate for the Pope. He spoke Latin, Arabic and Hebrew and was skilled in mathematics and medicine. But it was his translation of a book called *The Secret of Secrets* that led to his reputation for less academic and more spectacular talents. Thanks to his supposed feats of magic, such as the splitting of the Eildon Hills into three peaks, he came to be known as the Borders Wizard. He was also said to have prophetic abilities, although this proved to be a mixed blessing, as he foresaw the manner of his own death. Believing that he would die from being struck on the head by a small stone, he wore a steel helmet at all times, which he took off only in church. Inevitably, it was while he was in church that a stone fell from the ceiling and hit him on the head, and he died soon afterwards. It is believed that he was buried near a cross at Melrose Abbey, along with his books of magic.

'Harold, the peasants are revolting.'
'I know, M'lady. Even the dogs won't eat them.'

TWENTIETH-CENTURY CRISES

The Abyssinian Crisis, 1935

In October 1935, Italy invaded Abyssinia (now Ethiopia) and its ruler, Haile Selassie, appealed for help. However, Britain and France hesitated to condemn the invasion, as they were hoping to retain Mussolini as an ally against Hitler. The British and French foreign secretaries Sir Samuel Hoare and Pierre Laval instead drew up the Hoare-Laval pact, which proposed that Italy take half of Abyssinia. The pact was leaked, and a public outcry forced Hoare to resign.

TAKE ONE BOILED FROG

Remedies for common illnesses, as found in a tenth-century document

Back pain	Smoke from burned goat's hair
Baldness	Apply ashes of burned bees
Chilblains	Treat with eggs, fennel and wine
Headache	A stalk of crosswort tied to the head with a red scarf
Lack of virility	Agrimony boiled in milk
Shingles	A potion made from 15 types of bark
Spider bite	Fried and crushed black snails

20 *Thousands of pounds paid to the Vikings by Ethelred after the Battle of Maldon in 991*

Robin Hood is one of England's most popular legends, but historians have never been able to agree on who he might have been, or whether he existed at all. There have been many claimants to the title, but one of the more unusual of these is a twelfth century nobleman called David, Earl of Huntingdon (1152-1219).

The earliest reference to Robin Hood in English literature is in William Langland's poem *The vision of William concerning Piers Plowman*, written in 1377, in which Langland says:

'I do not know my paternoster perfectly as the priest sings it. But I know the rhymes of Robin Hood and Randolph, Earl of Chester.'

The Earl of Huntingdon was one of the leaders of the rebellion against King Henry II, which began in 1173, and one of his chief allies was Randolph, Earl of Chester. Huntingdon also later married Chester's sister, Matilda. It has often been noted that Robin Hood was not referred to as a nobleman until the sixteenth century, by playwright Anthony Munday. But while it is possible that Munday was elaborating on a romantic story, it is also likely that he was correcting a wrong done to Robin Hood in earlier Norman writings, in which the defender of the poor was portrayed as a common thief. Munday offered a further clue – in his play, Maid Marion's real name was Matilda.

Other theories have suggested that Robin Hood was a Yorkshireman, as some accounts of his life say he lived in Barnsdale, Yorkshire. But there was also a Barnsdale Wood in Rutland, much nearer to Robin Hood's traditional Nottingham. And it was owned by Huntingdon.

And there's more. Huntingdon was a close friend of Richard the Lionheart, and was one of the main supporters at his coronation. But there is no record of the Earl going on Crusades with the King – in fact, after Richard leaves for the Holy Lands, for the next four and a half years Huntingdon disappears completely from historical record. He does not reappear until the siege of Nottingham Castle in 1194, when he is seen at King Richard's side. Huntingdon and the Earl of Chester had been besieging the castle for two days before Richard arrived to take charge, and clearly had not been on the Crusades with their King. So it is possible that Richard left the Earl behind on purpose, to wage a secret war against Prince John and keep the kingdom safe from his clutches. And it had to be a secret war; had the Earl openly defied the Prince, it could have caused war between England and Scotland. Because the Earl of Huntingdon was not an English nobleman – he was the younger brother of King William II of Scotland. If this version of the legend is true, the quintessential English hero was in fact a Scot.

HISTORIC WORDS

What General Weygand called the Battle of France is over. I expect that the battle of Britain is about to begin. Upon this battle depends the survival of Christian civilisation. Upon it depends our own British life, and the long continuity of our institutions and our Empire. The whole fury and might of the enemy must very soon be turned on us. Hitler knows that he will have to break us in this island or lose the war. If we can stand up to him, all Europe may be free and the life of the world may move forward into broad, sunlit uplands. But if we fail, then the whole world, including the United States, including all that we have known and cared for, will sink into the abyss of a new dark age made more sinister, and perhaps more protracted, by the lights of perverted science. Let us therefore brace ourselves to our duties, and so bear ourselves that, if the British Empire and its Commonwealth last for a thousand years, men will still say, 'This was their finest hour.'

Winston Churchill, in a speech to the House of Commons, 18 June 1940

QUOTE UNQUOTE

English history is all about men liking their fathers, and American history is all about men hating their fathers and trying to burn down everything they ever did.
Malcolm Bradbury, novelist

THE LAST EXECUTION

The last people to be executed in the UK were Peter Anthony Allen and John Robson Walby on 13 August 1964. In 1965 the death penalty was suspended for five years, and then abolished in 1969, with an exception for treason and piracy with violence. A powerful factor in its abolition was the hanging of Derek Bentley, a 19-year-old man with a much younger mental age, whose 16-year-old friend shot and killed a policeman. It was claimed that Bentley had shouted 'Let him have it!' although it was also argued that he meant for his friend to give up his gun. A few years earlier a man named Timothy Evans had been hanged for murdering his wife and child, although it was later thought that convicted murderer John Christie might have been the culprit, as they had lived at the same house. The death penalty for all crimes was finally abolished in the UK in 1999.

The youngest person ever to be executed in Britain was an eight-year-old boy, hanged for arson in the 1600s. The last child to be executed in Britain was hanged in 1887, although the execution of children was not officially outlawed until 1933.

ROMAN PLACE NAMES

Modern name	Roman name
England	Albion
Ireland	Hibernia
Scotland	Caledonia
Wales	Cambria
Anglesey	Mona
Bath	Aquae Sulis
Cambridge	Granta
Canterbury	Durovernum
Carlisle	Luguvalium
Chelmsford	Caesaromagus
Chichester	Noviomagus
Colchester	Camulodonum
Doncaster	Danum
Dorchester	Durnovaria
Dover	Dubris
Exeter	Isca Dumnoniorum
Gloucester	Glevum
Great Yarmouth	Gernemuta Magna
Jersey	Caesaria
Lancaster	Lunecastrum
Leicester	Ratae
Lincoln	Lindum
Liverpool	Esmeduna
London	Londinium
Manchester	Mancunium
Newcastle	Pons Aelius
Salisbury	Sorviodunum
Southampton	Clausentum
Worcester	Vigornia
York	Eboracum

LESSER-KNOWN BRITISH ECCENTRICS

Edward Hyde, third Earl of Clarendon (1661-1723)

It has long been rumoured that when Edward Hyde was made governor of New Jersey by Queen Anne, he decided that as the representative of a Queen, he should conduct his job dressed as a woman, and turned up to his first function in a blue silk dress. Historians have since denounced the tale and blamed the Earl's enemies for spreading rumours of his transvestism (and those enemies did succeed in having him recalled to Britain). But to this day there hangs in the New York Historical Society a portrait of a very plain woman, who has never been identified; the only marking is the word 'Clarendon' scratched on to the frame.

A GROOVY KIND OF FAMINE

Throughout much of the Dark Ages, the poorest citizens dreaded the height of summer, as it brought the 'hungry gap', when those who could not afford to store grain, nor to buy others' stockpiled food, often went hungry. They existed on a meagre diet, usually including rye bread, which was invariably mouldy. The mould that grew on it was ergot, which gave the peasant a dose of lysergic acid – otherwise known as LSD. At best it would render them delirious; at worst it could kill. The poor also scavenged in the hedgerows for food, gathering poppies and hemp, which were ground up and baked in an early form of hash cake. The peasants knew what it did to them – it was referred to as 'crazy bread' – but they had little choice. The result, as contemporary historian Piers Plowman recorded, was a kind of mass hysteria expressed in over-excited summer festivals, fuelled by the peasants' unintentional drug-taking and the sheer lightheadedness of hunger.

PAST PUZZLES

Which king spent the least time in England?
Answer on page 153.

Answer on page 153.

IN THE BLEAK MIDWINTER

On 20 January 1838, London was in the grip of a deep freeze. On this, the coldest day, a thermometer in Hyde Park measured -3°F (-19°C) at 6.30am, and never got much above 18°F (-14°C) all day. Amid the freeze, one Patrick Murphy, a weather prophet, made his appearance. A month or two earlier he had submitted the manuscript of his *Weather Almanac on Scientific Principles Showing the State of the Weather for Every Day of the Year of 1838*. He had predicted that January would be particularly severe and that the twentieth of that month would most probably be the coldest day. When the accuracy of his prediction emerged, his publishers, Whittaker and Co, were inundated with requests for copies of the forthcoming book. Murphy made a tidy sum (although he later lost it just as quickly), even though by the end of the year he was found to have been right on only 167 days, and quite wrong on the rest. However, he based his predictions on his belief that the weather was dictated by the planets and stars. If he was wrong, he said, it was simply because the planets didn't do what they were supposed to do, for which he couldn't be held responsible. He continued to turn out the occasional weather almanac, none of which was any more accurate, until his death in 1847.

Year in 1900s when John Logie Baird was evicted from his lodgings after a failed experiment involving 12,000 volts of electricity

HISTORIC WORDS

The gentleness of the English civilization is perhaps its most marked characteristic. You notice it the instant you set foot on English soil. It is a land where the bus conductors are good-tempered and the policemen carry no revolvers. In no country inhabited by white men is it easier to shove people off the pavement. And with this goes something that is always written off by European observers as 'decadence' or hypocrisy, the English hatred of war and militarism. It is rooted deep in history, and it is strong in the lower-middle class as well as the working class. Successive wars have shaken it but not destroyed it. Well within living memory it was common for 'the redcoats' to be booed at in the streets and for the landlords of respectable public houses to refuse to allow soldiers on the premises. In peace time, even when there are two million unemployed, it is difficult to fill the ranks of the tiny standing army, which is officered by the county gentry and a specialized stratum of the middle class, and manned by farm labourers and slum proletarians. The mass of the people are without military knowledge or tradition, and their attitude towards war is invariably defensive. No politician could rise to power by promising them conquests or military 'glory', no Hymn of Hate has ever made any appeal to them. In the last war the songs which the soldiers made up and sang of their own accord were not vengeful but humorous and mock-defeatist. The only enemy they ever named was the sergeant-major.

George Orwell, *Why I Write*

ANGLO-SAXON DAYS OF THE WEEK

Monday	*Monan daeg*	Day of the moon
Tuesday	*Tiwes daeg*	Day of Tiw, god of war
Wednesday	*Wodnes daeg*	Day of Woden, chief god
Thursday	*Thorsdagr*	Day of Thor
Friday	*Frigedaeg*	Day of the goddess Frig, wife of Woden
Saturday	*Saeterdaeg*	Day of Saturn, Roman god of agriculture
Sunday	*Sunnan daeg*	Day of the sun

ETHELRED THE UNFAIRLY NAMED

King Ethelred's nickname of 'Ethelred the Unready' has always suggested that he was a war-shy king, or a leader who was more likely to drag his feet than make bold and kingly decisions. In fact his nickname was originally 'Unred', meaning 'ill-advised'. This was an unkind pun on 'Ethelred' which means 'of noble counsel' or 'well-advised'. Clearly the chroniclers of his time thought otherwise.

In 1839, a blacksmith from Dumfries named Kirkpatrick Macmillan invented the world's first bicycle. Known as a velocipede, it was made of a wooden frame, the front of which was carved into a horse's head, and it had iron-tyred wheels. It was propelled by two rods connected to the back wheel, which had to be pumped backwards and forwards. Despite the weight of the bicycle – 57lbs – Macmillan used it to get him the 14 miles from Dumfries to Courthill. His curious contraption led to the world's first cycling accident; when he cycled the 40 miles or so to Glasgow, a crowd turned out to see him and he accidentally knocked over a small child, for which he was fined five shillings.

THE YOUNG PRETENDERS

When Henry Tudor killed Richard III at the Battle of Bosworth in 1485, he claimed the throne on the grounds that he was a descendant of Edward III. This tenuous route to succession left Henry open to alternative claims upon the throne, the first of which came from a boy named Lambert Simnel.

Simnel landed in Ireland in 1487, claiming that he was the Earl of Warwick, Richard III's nephew, and had recently escaped from the Tower. He found willing supporters in Ireland, who crowned him king there, and plotted to place him on the English throne.

Simnel and his supporters launched a half-hearted invasion, but were easily defeated at the Battle of Stoke. Simnel was captured, and the real Earl of Warwick was temporarily removed from the Tower and paraded in public to dispel any confusion.

However, King Henry was so unthreatened by the incompetent claimant (not least because Simnel was barely 12 years old) that he put him to work in the royal kitchens, where it is alleged he invented a particularly delicious fruit cake that still bears his name. However, this is more likely to be coincidence than truth.

The second claimant had the equally unlikely name of Perkin Warbeck, who claimed to be Richard, Duke of York, the youngest of the famous princes imprisoned in the Tower. Warbeck took the precaution of securing the support of the Scottish king, James IV, and a group of English nobles attempting to steal the throne. James IV began an invasion of England on Warbeck's behalf, but later expelled the pretender in fear of retaliation.

But it seemed that all the attention had gone to Warbeck's head, and he besieged Exeter in 1497. He was defeated, then later captured and was executed in 1499.

Number of goals scored by Preston North End in 1887, the biggest FA Cup victory ever recorded. The other team, Hyde United, scored 0

OLD PICTURE, NEW CAPTION

Edith discovers the downside of equal rights for women.

HISTORIC FIGURES COCKNEY-STYLE

Captain Cook *book*
Doctor Crippen *dripping*
Jack the Ripper *kipper*
Molly Malone *phone*
Oliver Twist *fist*
Richard the Third *bird*

SHOOTING THE MESSENGER

In the thirteenth century, King Henry III struggled to exert power over the tribal princes of Wales, and came to various arrangements with them, in which he promised to leave them alone in return for the use of their men as troops. However, not everyone was receptive to his diplomacy. When Henry sent a summons to Walter de Clifford, Lord of Llandovery, de Clifford was so outraged by the King's presumption of authority over him that he forced the messenger to eat the summons – royal seal and all.

In the year 122, the Emperor Hadrian decided to build an immense wall across the north of Britain, to divide the Roman-occupied territories in the south from unoccupied Caledonia to the north, where the Caledonian tribes remained unsubdued. Legionaries from the IInd Augusta, XXth Valeria Victrix and VIIth Victrix began to build the wall in 122, and took about 16 years to complete the task.

The wall ran for 80 Roman miles from Wallsend in the east to Bowness-on-Solway in the west. It was intended at first to be a series of signal stations, but ended up as a continuous wall with 16 forts (permanent quarters for garrisons), milecastles every mile for patrols and signal towers in between. It measured around eight feet deep and 15-20 feet high, and was protected by a ditch on its northern side and a flat-bottomed trench to the south. It was guarded by a garrison of around 20,000 soldiers. Parts of it were destroyed during various uprisings, but it was rebuilt by the Romans each time.

After the Romans left, the wall was often plundered for building materials, and much of it was destroyed during the construction of a major road from Newcastle to Carlisle in the 1750s. Since then it has enjoyed better protection and is now looked after by various bodies such as the National Trust and English Heritage. It is much visited by ramblers, although few have matched the endeavours of one William Hutton from Birmingham, who in 1801 walked its entire length at the age of 79 and wrote a book about its history.

QUOTE UNQUOTE

Byron! – he would be all forgotten today if he had lived to be a florid old gentleman with iron-grey whiskers, writing very long, very able letters to The Times *about the Repeal of the Corn Laws.*
Max Beerbohm, writer and caricaturist

THE COUNTIES OF 1086

The counties surveyed in the *Domesday Book*, in order of appearance
Kent • Sussex • Surrey • Hampshire (with the Isle of Wight)
Berkshire • Wiltshire • Dorset • Somerset • Devon • Cornwall
Middlesex • Hertfordshire • Buckinghamshire • Oxfordshire
Gloucestershire • Worcestershire • Herefordshire
Cambridgeshire • Huntingdonshire • Bedfordshire
Northamptonshire • Leicestershire • Warwickshire • Staffordshire,
Shropshire • Cheshire (with part of Lancashire) • Derbyshire,
Nottinghamshire (with part of Rutland) • Yorkshire • Lincolnshire

GREAT BRITONS

Captain James Cook (1728-1779)

Captain Cook was one of the world's greatest explorers. Born in Yorkshire, he was apprenticed to a shopkeeper, but left his post for the more exciting life of a sailor. After gaining experience on trading vessels, he joined the Navy and in 1759 was given the difficult task of charting the channel of the St Lawrence River in Canada, an experience that was to prove invaluable. In 1766, Cook was commissioned by the government to sail to the Pacific and observe the transit of Venus, and he set off in 1768 on the first of his three great voyages. He sailed around Cape Horn to discover New Zealand and on to the east coast of Australia, which he claimed for King George III. He returned home via New Guinea and the Cape, although the journey was blighted by dysentery and malaria among his crew. In 1772, Cook set sail again, this time for New Zealand via the Antarctic, sailing back to and around the South Pole before returning home in 1775, crossing a greater expanse of sea than any man had before. His third voyage, in 1776, took him past New Zealand and on around the world to America. After further expeditions to the Arctic Circle, Cook returned to Hawaii, where the natives were at first welcoming. But then trouble broke out and in a scuffle on the beach, Cook was stabbed in the back by one of the natives and fell dead. His body was dismembered by the natives, but his crew demanded that they return his remains, and they buried what was left of him at sea. Despite his historic and courageous achievements, Cook described himself simply as 'a plain man, zealously exerting himself in the service of his country'.

FIREFIGHTING

The first fire insurance company in Britain was started in an office in Threadneedle Street, London, by a man with the unlikely name of If-Jesus-Christ-had-not-died-for-thee-thou-hadst-been-damned Barebones, the son of the Parliamentarian Praise-God Barebones. Barebones Junior left his original profession of physician and, changing his name to Nicholas Barbon, moved into the building trade when the Great Fire of London in 1666 opened up new opportunities. Having made his fortune, Barbon ventured into the world of fire insurance, setting up the Phenix Fire Office in 1680. He also formed the world's first fire brigade in 1684, which protected the houses he insured. The untrained firemen were paid one shilling for the first hour and 6d for subsequent hours of firefighting, as well as all the beer they required. The business operated successfully until it was eventually wound up in 1712.

To-day was the first day of the general strike. Many more motors about. I walked round to Victoria, which was shut up (both stations) one small entrance guarded by policemen. I heard someone say that a train had gone somewhere during the morning. Yet in the vast empty station Smith's bookstalls were open. So were (outside) the cafes. The populace excited and cheery, on this 1st day of the strike. No evening paper. News from the Wireless at very short intervals, 1/2 hour intervals at night up to midnight. I should think that nearly all theatres would soon be closed. Already to-day there has been a noticeably increasing gravity in the general demeanour.

From the diary of Arnold Bennett, 4 May 1926.
The nationwide strike by trade unionists lasted from 4 to 12 May

FAMOUS HORSES IN HISTORY

Horse	Rider
Black Agnes	Mary Queen of Scots
Black Bess	Dick Turpin
Copenhagen	Duke of Wellington
Lamri	King Arthur
Ronald	Lord Cardigan
Rosabelle	Mary Queen of Scots
Sorrel	William III
White Surrey	Richard III

BRITAIN'S LAST STAND

The last battle fought on British soil was at Culloden Field, near Inverness on 16 April 1746, between Charles Stuart (Bonnie Prince Charlie, the Young Pretender) and the forces of King George II. The Jacobite rebels were defeated and the would-be king fled, disguised as a woman, having failed to restore the Stuarts to the throne.

The last battle fought on English soil was the Battle of Sedgemoor in Somerset, fought on 6 July 1685, when the forces of James II defeated those of the Duke of Monmouth, the illegitimate son of Charles II.

The last clan battle in Scotland was that between Clan Mackintosh and Clan MacDonald at Mulroy in 1688.

The bloodiest battle fought between the British on their own soil was the Battle of Towton in Yorkshire on 29 March 1461, when 36,000 Yorkists defeated 42,000 Lancastrians. The death toll is thought to have been around 28,000.

FAMOUS LAST WORDS

The parting words of some historic figures

What dost thou fear? Strike man, strike!
Sir Walter Raleigh, courtier, explorer and adventurer, to his executioner in 1618.

There are six guineas for you. And do not hack me as you did my Lord Russell.
Duke of Monmouth, the illegitimate son of Charles II, to his executioner in 1685.

It's all been very interesting.
Lady Mary Wortley Montagu, writer, feminist, socialite. Died 1762.

Too late for fruit, too soon for flowers.
Walter de la Mare, poet, on being asked if he would like fruit or flowers. Died 1956.

So now all is gone. Empire, body, soul.
King Henry VIII. Died 1547.

The devil do with it! It will end as it began; it came with a lass and it will go with a lass.
James V, King of Scotland. Died 1542.

Either that wallpaper goes, or I do.
Oscar Wilde, wit and dramatist Died 1900.

Be of good cheer, Master Ridley, and play the man. We shall this day light such a candle, by God's grace, in England, as I trust shall never be put out.
Hugh Latimer, Bishop of Worcester, to Nicholas Ridley, Bishop of London, both burned at the stake by Mary I in 1555.

PAST PUZZLE

What was the Alexandra limp?
Answer on page 153.

HOW MONEY WAS MADE

In the year 1000 there were about 70 mints around England, producing soft silver alloy coins for public use. However, there was a catch; the coins were valid for only two or three years, and then they had to be taken back and exchanged for new ones. For every 10 that were handed in, you received only eight or nine in return, and the rest was kept by the government. The money-exchanger was therefore an early kind of tax-collector and sometimes, in more provincial areas, he also made the coins. He could have made more money by adding more alloy to the silver, but as the penalty for such fraud was to have his hand cut off and nailed to the wall of the mint, the temptation was easily resisted.

Number of people killed by lightning in the UK in 1914, the worst   31
year on record

The most famous plague in British history was the Black Death, possibly the greatest tragedy ever to hit western Europe. It began in Asia and was spread by rats who stowed away on the trading ships that linked Asia to Europe. This bubonic (glandular) plague soon ripped across the medieval world, reaching the south coast of Britain in 1348. Two of the first victims were Edward III's daughter, Joan, who died in Bordeaux in September of that year, and the Archbishop of Canterbury, who died a month earlier, proving that no one was safe. Nobility and peasantry alike were felled in their thousands. In the first year, the plague killed one-fifth of the entire population of Britain, and would eventually dispatch almost half the country. Worldwide, it claimed the lives of 75,000,000 people.

The illness struck quickly; black boils erupted under the skin in the groin and armpits, and sufferers were dead within a few days or hours. Men and women dropped dead in the street, and entire towns and cities were wiped out in days or weeks. The disease was so contagious that the healthy were forced to abandon the sick in order to survive, and families and communities were torn apart. Modern excavations of burial grounds show that bodies were simply piled into pits five or six deep and covered over, without ceremony. In a short-sighted tactic, the Scots saw an opportunity to launch an attack on the English, and gathered at Selkirk forest. But plague struck the camp, 5,000 died, and the rest returned to Scotland, taking the disease with them. Even as the plague died down, the horror was not yet over. It returned in 1362, 1369 and 1375 to carry off the survivors of the first wave. Before 1348, the population of Britain was about 5,000,000; by the end of the century it was around 3,500,000 or less. The population of Britain did not recover until the middle of the next century.

However, despite all the devastation, the plague did bring about changes that were of considerable benefit to the survivors. A shortage of labour meant that those who were left were in a strong position for negotiation; wages sometimes doubled, especially for farmhands who were producing food for what was left of the population. Landowners desperate for tenants had to improve their terms, and serfs who had previously worked for nothing now demanded wages and, eventually, their freedom. Many men who had been farming a tiny plot of land inherited the plots left by their dead relations, and found they were wealthy. The peasants also lost some of their respect for authority, not least because they had seen how readily the nobility and clergy had fled to safety, abandoning their tenants and flock. The plague would return with depressing regularity in the decades to come, but after this one terrible outbreak, things would never be quite the same again.

THEY SAY IT'LL BE OVER BY CHRISTMAS

The longest wars in which Britain fought
The Hundred Years War lasted 116 years, from 1337-1453
The Wars of the Roses lasted 30 years, from 1455-1485
The Thirty Years War lasted 30 years, from 1618-1648
The Napoleonic Wars lasted 23 years, from 1792-1815

HISTORIC WORDS

Lines written in the Highlands after a visit to Burns's Country
There is a joy in footing slow across a silent plain,
Where patriot battle has been fought when glory had the gain;
There is a pleasure on the heath where Druids old have been,
Where mantles grey have rustled by and swept the nettles green;
There is a joy in every spot made known by times of old,
New to the feet, although the tale a hundred times be told;
There is a deeper joy than all, more solemn in the heart,
More parching to the tongue than all, of more divine a smart,
When weary steps forget themselves upon a pleasant turf,
Upon hot sand, or flinty road, or sea-shore iron scurf,
Toward the castle or the cot, where long ago was born
One who was great through mortal days, and died of fame unshorn.
John Keats, English Romantic poet

QUOTE UNQUOTE

*The very first requirement in a hospital is
that it should do the sick no harm.*
Florence Nightingale, a pioneer of cleanliness in hospitals

A DAY AT THE RACES

In 2005, a building company digging up a site in Colchester, Essex
unearthed the remains of a Roman chariot-racing arena that dated back
to around 50AD. Measuring 400 metres long by 60 metres wide, it was
large enough to accommodate up to 8,000 spectators. Historians believe
that the riders would have had to complete about seven laps around the
arena, which was two miles of racing. As well as the basic outline of the
arena, archaeologists found pieces of horse trapping, horse jaws, a man's
skeleton, a Roman coin and a stylus, which might have been used to
write down bets. It is the largest Roman building in Britain, and apart
from a similar complex found in Germany, it is the only large chariot-
racing complex to have been found in northern Europe.

*Length, in feet, of each of the three sides of the Triangular Lodge in 33
Northamptonshire, built in 1597*

1553 The first queen to rule alone is crowned: Mary I 'Bloody Mary'. (Henry I declared his daughter Matilda his heir and she took control of the country for a few months in 1141, but was never crowned. Lady Jane Grey was declared queen in 1553, but was deposed within nine days and was never crowned.)

1903 The Women's Social and Political Union is founded by Emmeline Pankhurst and her daughters Christabel and Sylvia.

1909 Elizabeth Garrett Anderson is elected Mayor of Aldeburgh, Suffolk, and is the first woman to become mayor.

1918 Women are given the vote (if aged 30 and over).

1918 The first year in which women could be elected as MPs.

1918 Constance, Countess Markiewicz, is the first woman to be elected to Parliament. Elected MP for Sinn Fein, she was unable to take her seat, as she was in prison.

1919 The first woman takes her seat in the House of Commons: Nancy Astor, the Conservative MP for Plymouth South.

1928 The voting age is made the same for women and men for the first time.

1929 Margaret Bondfield becomes the first woman to be a Cabinet Minister; she is appointed Minister for Labour in the Labour minority government.

1955 Dame Evelyn Sharp becomes the first woman to be head of a department in the Civil Service.

1979 Margaret Thatcher, Conservative, becomes the UK's first female Prime Minister.

1992 Betty Boothroyd, appointed on 27 April, is the first woman to be made Speaker of the House of Commons.

THE FIRST DIVORCE

The first civil divorce in England was granted in 1546, to separate a Lady Sadleir of Standon, Hertfordshire, from her first husband, Mr Barr. Formerly Mrs Margaret Barr, Lady Sadleir had remarried after Barr disappeared and was presumed dead, but he inconveniently reappeared after his wife had married Sir Ralph Sadleir. The Ecclesiastical Courts were alarmed; the second marriage could not be confirmed until the first was dissolved, and was clearly bigamous. Fortunately they gave Lady Sadleir the benefit of the doubt and accepted that she had remarried in good faith, but they had to go to the considerable lengths of putting a Private Bill through Parliament to allow her first marriage to be dissolved. It was to be the only civil divorce granted to a woman before 1801.

34 *Cost, in thousands of pounds sterling, of the construction of Marble Arch*

THE IMPERIAL SIZE OF A FIELD

1 square mile = 640 acres
1 acre = 10 sq chains = 4 roods
1 rood = 40 sq poles
1 sq pole = 30 1/4 sq yards
1 sq yard = 9 sq feet
1 sq foot = 144 sq inches

HISTORIC WORDS

If I should die, think only this of me:
That there's some corner of a foreign field
That is for ever England. There shall be
In that rich earth a richer dust concealed;
A dust whom England bore, shaped, made aware,
Gave, once, her flowers to love, her ways to roam,
A body of England's, breathing English air,
Washed by the rivers, blest by suns of home.
And think, this heart, all evil shed away,
A pulse in the eternal mind, no less
Gives somewhere back the thoughts by England given;
Her sights and sounds; dreams happy as her day;
And laughter, learnt of friends; and gentleness,
In hearts at peace, under an English heaven.

Rupert Brooke, *The Soldier*
The poet died on the way to Gallipoli in 1915

PRIDE BEFORE A FALL

The world's first traffic island was thought up by a Colonel
Pierpoint, who had it constructed outside his London club on
St James's Street in 1864. He would often turn to admire it as he
crossed, which caused him on one occasion to be knocked down by
a car while heading for his club.

THE COST OF WAR

Estimated figures for World Wars One and Two*

Number of British combatants killed in World War One 743,000
Number of British combatants killed in World War Two.....468,000
Total combatant death toll of Word War One,
all countries 15,000,000
Total combatant death toll of World War Two,
all countries 65,000,000

Based on the best estimates. The true cost may never be known.

OLD PICTURE, NEW CAPTION

Lady Fortescue was delighted to find that her new lorgnettes added a good 50 yards to her chaperoning range.

QUOTE UNQUOTE

The disadvantage of men not knowing the past is that they do not know the present. History is a hill or high point of vantage, from which alone men see the town in which they live or the age in which they are living.
GK Chesterton, author

BRITISH RECORD-BREAKERS

Britain's tallest man:	Patrick Cotter O'Brien (1760-1806) from County Cork: eight feet one inch. He was officially a giant, being over eight feet tall.
Tallest Scotsman:	Angus Macaskill (1825-63) from Berneray in the Sound of Harris: seven feet nine inches.
Tallest Englishman:	William Bradley (1787-1820) born in Market Weighton, East Yorkshire: seven feet nine inches.
Tallest Welshman:	William Evans (1599-1634) of Gwent, porter to King James I: seven feet six inches.

Age of Daniel Lambert, England's fattest man, when he died in 1806, weighing 52 stone

The Battle of Rorke's Drift, which took place on 22 and 23 January 1879, is one of history's most stirring conflicts, where victory was achieved in the face of overwhelming odds, thanks to the initiative and sheer courage of the soldiers involved.

When General Lord Chelmsford invaded Zululand, he left behind B Company of the 24th (2nd Warwickshire) Regiment of Foot to guard the Buffalo River crossing at Rorke's Drift. The encampment consisted of a store, a chapel, a temporary hospital and around 150 men.

In command was Lieutenant Gonville Bromhead of the 24th. However, when Prince Dabulamanzikampande ignored the orders of the King and attacked the post with about 4,500 Zulus, it was an officer of the Royal Engineers, Lieutenant John Chard, who took command.

Being an engineer, Chard had a good eye for defences and quickly constructed barricades with sacks of corn and an inner barricade made of biscuit boxes. The Zulus attacked head on, wielding their short stabbing assegais, but were unable to reach the men behind the barricades and were blasted by the famous British Infantry rapid rifle-fire, at point blank range. Most of those who did mount the breastwork were killed by the bayonets of the defenders.

After a number of unsuccessful attacks, the Zulus set fire to the hospital by shooting fire arrows into the thatch, trapping the patients, so Private Henry Hook kept the enemy at bay with his bayonet while Private John Williams hacked holes in the mud walls separating one room from another and dragged the patients through one by one.

Fighting went on all night in the fitful glare from the blazing hospital, as the Zulus made charge after charge. One patient, Corporal Christian Ferdinand Schiess, stabbed three Zulus in quick succession despite being on crutches. In the open air, Surgeon James Reynolds tended to the wounded, despite the life and death struggle going on all around him. Those too badly hurt to shoot reloaded the guns, and resupplied ammunition to those who were still on their feet.

When dawn came at last, the Zulus retreated, taking their wounded with them and leaving about 350 dead in front of the barricades.

Lieutenants Chard and Bromhead were both awarded the Victoria Cross, as were nine others, including Dalton, Hook, Reynolds, Williams and Schiess, the first member of the South African volunteer forces to win a Victoria Cross. The regiment – now the South Wales Borders – has always been proud to claim '11 VCs before breakfast'. In truth the medals were won by eight men from the 2nd Warwickshire, a Royal Engineer, a surgeon from the Army Hospital Corps and a Natal Volunteer.

THE WAGES OF SIN

Laura Bell, a former shop assistant from Belfast, could arguably claim the title of London's most expensive prostitute. In 1850 she charged the prime minister to the Maharaja of Nepal £250,000 to spend one night with her. He paid up. She later married the nephew of the Bishop of Norwich and became a preacher. She was preceded in her profession by the equally bold Kitty Fisher, whose nightly fee was 100 guineas, and who once threw the Duke of York out of bed for trying to pay her with a mere £50 note. She baked the note in a pie and ate it for breakfast. She finally embraced respectability by marrying an MP in 1765.

HISTORIC WORDS

In London there is great outrage about our radio broadcasts in English. Our announcer has been given the nickname 'Lord Haw-Haw'. He is causing talk, and that is already half the battle. The aim in London is to create an equivalent figure for the German service. This would be the best thing that could happen. We should make mincemeat of him.

Joseph Goebbels, from his diary, 5 January 1918

WITCHES, PROPHETS AND MYSTIC MEN

Robert Nixon

To most people, Robert Nixon seemed like a simpleton. Gangly and almost mute, with an enlarged head and bulging eyes, he was an odd addition to the Cholmondeley household of 1485, capable only of ploughing their fields. But Robert had a special talent – he could predict the future. His first predictions were simple ones, such as the death of a neighbour's ox. But he soon began to work on a grander scale and predicted the Great Plague, the 1666 fire of London, the beheading of Charles I, the reign of William of Orange and the French Revolution. His only fear seemed to be that his employers would starve him to death – he had a vast appetite and had to be watched in case he ate himself sick. When Robert predicted the defeat of Richard III at the Battle of Bosworth two days before it happened, his genius reached the ears of the new king, Henry VII. The king sent for Robert and gave him a scribe to write down his predictions. Sadly, before the king could actually meet his new prophet, Robert's greatest fear was realised; a furious cook, tired of finding the boy stealing food, locked him in a cupboard and forgot about him. His body was found two weeks later.

THE INFLUENZA PANDEMIC

The most severe epidemic to hit the UK in the twentieth century was an outbreak of influenza, which began in 1918. The Spanish flu, as it was called, swept across the world, killing young and old, strong and weak alike. The US and India suffered the highest mortality rates, and the healthy seemed to succumb to the illness more quickly than the weak, putting paid to the suggestion that it spread because its victims had been weakened by the deprivations of World War One. The outbreak killed around 200,000 people in Britain and about 10,000 British servicemen.

BRITAIN'S ROYAL ASTRONOMERS

John Flamsteed *1675-1719*
Edmund Halley *1720-1742*
James Bradley *1742-1762*
Nathaniel Bliss *1762-1764*
Nevil Maskelyne *1765-1811*
John Pond *1811-1835*
Sir George Airy *1835-1881*
Sir William Christie *1881-1910*
Sir Frank Dyson *1910-1933*
Sir Harold Jones *1933-1955*
Sir Richard Woolley *1956-1971*
Sir Martin Ryle *1972-1982*
Sir Francis Graham-Smith *1982-1990*
Sir Arnold Wolfendale *1991-1995*
Sir Martin Rees *1995*

TWENTIETH-CENTURY CRISES

The Chanak Crisis, 1922

In September 1922, the British government became concerned that Mustapha Kemal (Ataturk) of Turkey would attack the Allied armies guarding the approach to Istanbul (then Constantinople). Kemal had recently defeated the Greeks at Smyrna, and the fear was that he would try to reclaim territory assigned to the Greeks in the 1920 Treaty of Sevres, a treaty he had never accepted. The Prime Minister, Lloyd George, wanted to strengthen British forces serving at Chanak; but the crisis was avoided by an Anglo-Turkish agreement made in October that returned certain territories to Turkey, in return for its agreement not to pursue further territorial ambitions. The crisis, and the closeness of war with Turkey was the downfall of Lloyd George, who found himself out of office two weeks after the agreement was signed.

THE FIRST PRIME MINISTERS OF BRITAIN

1721	Sir Robert Walpole
1742	Earl of Wilmington
1743	Henry Pelham
1754	Duke of Newcastle
1756	Duke of Devonshire
1757	Duke of Newcastle
1762	Earl of Bute
1763	George Grenville
1765	Marquis of Rockingham
1766	Earl of Chatham
1768	Duke of Grafton
1770	Lord North

QUOTE UNQUOTE

Swindon: What will History say?
Burgoyne: History, sir, will tell lies, as usual.
George Bernard Shaw, *The Devil's Disciple*

STRANGE CUSTOMS

Red Hose Race

In Carwath in Strathclyde every August, a race is run in which all the participants have to wear red woollen stockings. The tradition dates back to 1508, when King James IV granted the lands and barony of Carnwath to Lord Somerville. The terms of the grant stated that the owner of Carnwath must, as part of his rent, pay 'one pair of hose containing half an ell of English cloth at the feast of Saint John the Baptist called Midsummer, to the man running most quickly from the east end of the town of Carnwath to the cross called Cawlo Cross'. While this may seem like a mischievous forfeit, it may have had something to do with training messengers to give warnings of raids on their border, although that doesn't explain why they didn't do so on horseback. The tradition has been continued ever since, as the estate would in theory be forfeited if this 'rent' were not paid. During the two world wars and the Foot and Mouth outbreaks of 1926 and 1952, permission had to be secured in writing from the Crown Authorities for the race to be suspended. Some details of the race have changed over the years; the distance has been reduced from three miles to one and it is held in August rather than mid-summer. And instead of the waist-high blue cloth hose that was specified in the original grant, the runners now wear red woollen tights, knitted by the villagers.

Height, in feet, of the main entrance doors of Fonthill Abbey

PAST PUZZLE

What will the following phrase help you to remember?
Can Queen Victoria Eat Cold Apple Pie?
Answer on page 153.

FOR THE WIPING OF ONE'S NOSE

Next time you blow your nose, you can thank Richard II, as it was he who was credited with bringing the handkerchief to England. His wardrobe accounts were in Latin, but when transcribed, they described this peculiar new affectation as: 'Made of small pieces for the Lord King to carry in his hand for wiping and cleaning his nose.' It took a while to catch on and did not find favour for another hundred years or so. Richard, with an eye to the niceties of life, also introduced the novelties of individual, rather than communal, toilets and small fireplaces in the rooms of his courtiers.

HOW MANY PECKS IN A BUSHEL?

The dry measure weights that time forgot
1 chaldron = 36 bushels
1 quarter = 8 bushels
1 bushel = 4 pecks
1 peck = 2 gallons
1 gallon = 4 quarts
1 quart = 2 pints
1 pint = 4 gills

THE EARLIEST ATKINS

The first formal slimming diet known in the UK was devised in 1862 by a Dr Harvey, for an overweight undertaker named William Banting. The diet consisted of the following:

Breakfast   4oz lean meat, fish or bacon; 1 oz toast
Dinner   A little more meat; vegetables (not potatoes), fruit, 1 oz toast
Tea   Tea without milk, a rusk, fruit
Supper   4oz meat or fish

This low-carbohydrate diet was not dissimilar to the famous Atkins diet, and it worked very nicely for Banting; within a year he had reduced his weight from 203lbs to 153lbs and extolled the virtues of the diet to anyone who would listen. His success gave rise to a new verb 'to bant', meaning to lose weight. But, unlike the practice of dieting, the word soon fell out of fashion.

HATS OFF

The bowler hat was invented in 1849 by Thomas and William Bowler, felt hatmakers of Southwark Bridge Road to fulfil an order placed by Lock & Co of St James's. William Coke of Holkham, Norfolk, a customer of Lock & Co, was in need of a hat that would protect his head from overhanging branches while he was out shooting and Lock & Co commissioned the Bowlers to solve the problem. When Coke travelled to London on 17 December 1849 to collect his hat, he placed it on the ground and stamped on it firmly, twice, to test its resilience. The hat was undamaged, and Coke paid his 12 shillings. Although the rest of the world refers to the hat as a bowler, Lock & Co still refer to it as a Coke.

SCHOOL'S OUT

The age at which a child could leave school in the UK

1870	10 years
1899	12 years
1918	14 years
1944	15 years
1973	16 years

Other educational milestones

1870 Education provided for all children over five.
1880 School attendance made compulsory.
1891 State education provided free of charge.
1944 Education divided into primary and secondary levels.
1944 Eleven-plus exam introduced.
1965 Comprehensive schools first established.
1988 National Curriculum drawn up (revised in 1994).

STRANGE CUSTOMS

The Boys' Ploughing Match, Orkney

This centuries-old contest has its roots in Norse tradition – Orkney remained under Danish rule until well into the Middle Ages. On the third Saturday in August, on the tiny island of South Ronaldsay, boys and girls dress up as horses in traditional costume, which has often been passed down through the generations. After the horse costumes have been judged, the 'ploughmen' – boys under the age of 15 – line up on the beach at the Sands O'Right with their miniature ploughs, again often family heirlooms, and compete for the best furrow ploughed in the sand. The results are judged very solemnly with points given for straightest line, neatest ends and best starts.

Frank wondered how long it would take Agatha to realise that there was no such game as Strip Patience.

QUOTE UNQUOTE

He speaks to Me as if I was a public meeting.
Queen Victoria, of Prime Minister William Gladstone

THE TROUBLE WITH MERCENARIES

After the Romans departed in 409, Britain's various kings were once again left to protect their own territories. According to legend, one such king, Vortigern, made the mistake of hiring mercenaries to do his fighting for him, not imagining that they might get a taste for their spoils. The most famous of these were the brothers Hengist and Horsa. Vortigern was impressed by their work and granted them the Isle of Thanet in place of the 'wages' he had promised. Furious, they rampaged through Britain, collecting their own rewards. Having lost his grip, Vortigern was then overthrown by his own son and sent into exile. Which just goes to show that it pays to fight your own battles.

MURDERED MONARCHS

Edmund I Killed during a fight at a feast in 946.

Duff of Scotland Killed in 954 in Moray.

Edward the Martyr Killed in 978 by supporters of his younger half-brother, Ethelred.

Edmund II, 'Ironside' Killed in 1016, probably by supporters of Canute.

Malcolm III of Scotland Ambushed in 1093 by the Earl of Northumberland.

William II Killed in 1100 by an arrow, while out hunting.

Edward II Killed in Berkeley Castle in 1327, on the orders of his wife Isabella and her lover.

Richard II Killed at Pontefract Castle in 1400 after being deposed by Henry IV in 1399.

James I (Scotland) Killed by assassins in 1437.

Henry VI Killed in 1471 at prayer in the Tower of London, possibly by the future Richard III.

Edward V Murdered in 1483 at the age of 12, probably on the orders of Richard III.

James III (Scotland) Killed in 1488, after the royal army was defeated at Sauchieburn.

Lady Jane Grey Executed in 1553 after nine days as queen.

Charles I Tried and executed in 1649.

HISTORIC WORDS

As the fire spread rapidly through the houses the people who had been rejoicing in the church were thrown into confusion, and a crowd of men and women of every rank and status, compelled by this disaster rushed out of the church. Only the bishops and the clergy along with the monks stayed, terrified, in front of the altar and only just managed to complete the consecration rite over the king who was trembling violently. Nearly everyone else ran towards the raging fire, some to fight bravely against the force of the flames, but more hoping to grab loot for themselves amid such great confusion. The English, believing there was a plot behind something so completely unlooked for, were extremely angry and afterwards held the Normans in suspicion, judging them treacherous.

An account by the historian Orderic Vitalis of the disrupted coronation of William the Conqueror, 25 December 1066
The fire was started by the guards outside who, hearing shouts of acclaim from inside Westminster Cathedral, assumed a fight had started and set fire to the surrounding buildings (a standard tactic).

OFF WITH THEIR HEADS

In early 2005, 56 skeletons were found in a Roman cemetery in York. The find itself was not unusual, but what puzzled archaeologists was that the skeletons' heads had been chopped off, despite the fact that the Romans had no tradition of decapitation. They concluded that the dead men may have been soldiers from what is now the Rhineland in Germany, who served under Emperor Septimus Severus in 200AD, and who had been buried according to tribal tradition, with their displaced skulls placed by their feet or legs. Dr Patrick Ottaway of the York Archaeological Trust said: 'Romans believed that the head was the seat of the soul, and they may have cut off their heads to stop them haunting the living.'

HOW TO MEASURE YOUR PINT OF ALE

How we measured liquid before the litre

1 tun = 2 butts
1 butt = 2 hogsheads
1 hogshead = 1 1/2 barrels
1 barrel = 2 kilderkins
1 kilderkin = 2 firkins
1 firkin = 9 gallons
1 gallon = 4 quarts
1 quart = 2 pints
1 pint = 4 gills
1 gill = 5 fluid ounces
1 fluid ounce = 8 fluid drachms
1 fluid drachms = 60 minims

YORKSHIRE ROCK

Britain's famous Blackpool rock was first made not in Blackpool but in Yorkshire. In 1876, former miner Ben Bullock, who had set up in Dewsbury as a confectioner, came up with the idea of making a stick of sweet rock with words running through it. The first words he used were 'Whoa Emma', a popular music hall song of the time. He took some rock on holiday to Blackpool, and when it attracted the attention of local merchants, he made up a quantity of rock containing the word 'Blackpool'. Orders soon flooded in from home and overseas, and a great British tradition was born. Blackpool rock has continued to be part of our heritage, with only one small hiccup; a 1970s report on industrial sabotage told the sad tale of a consignment of rock that had to be thrown away when it was discovered that a four-letter obscenity ran through the centre of each stick, the work of a disgruntled employee.

THE POWER OF SUPERSTITION

Had the Roman legions of 43AD given in to their irrational fears, the history of Britain might have been very different. At the time of the Roman invasion, the wisest minds insisted that the continent the Romans inhabited was surrounded by empty oceans. For a land mass to rise out of the water, which is how Britain was perceived, suggested that the island they sought to occupy was something mysterious, and perhaps not to be interfered with. So despite Julius Caesar's short foray into British territory in 55BC, the troops were unhappy. In 40AD, the Emperor Gaius assembled an invading army, but the army refused to sail. It was only three years later, after a near mutiny, that the soldiers of Aulus Plautius agreed to venture into the unknown and landed on the shores of first century Britain.

THOSE WHOM THE GODS LOVE...

Creative spirits who died too young

Thomas Chatterton, *poet*	17
John Keats, *poet*	25
Aubrey Beardsley, *artist*	25
Percy Bysshe Shelley, *poet*	29
Wilfred Owen, *poet*	25
Rupert Brooke, *poet*	27
Anne Brontë, *novelist*	29
Christopher Marlowe, *playwright*	29

QUOTE, UNQUOTE

We are not interested in the possibilities of defeat; they do not exist.
Queen Victoria, during the 'Black Week' of the Boer War

CAR TROUBLE

The first man to drive a motor car on public roads in the UK was Henry Hewetson of Catford, who purchased a 2hp Benz from Mannheim and brought it home in November 1894. He drove around Catford for several weeks before being stopped by the police and informed that his automobile did not conform with the Locomotives on Highways Act 1865, which required him to have a man walking ahead of the car, waving a red flag. Infuriated by such petty rules, Hewetson employed two boys, one to travel in the car and one to go ahead by bicycle and keep an eye out for policeman. When an officer was spotted, the first boy signalled to the second boy, who hopped out of the car and strolled along in front of it, holding up a two-inch square of red linen attached to a small pencil.

46 *Height, in centimetres, of undersized courtier Jeffrey Hudson when he jumped out of a pie baked for Charles I*

GREAT BRITISH FIRSTS

1809	Britain's first letter box is installed in Wakefield, set into the wall of a post office.
1814	The UK's first art gallery opens, the Dulwich College Picture Gallery in London.
1825	A blood transfusion saves a life for the first time in the UK.
1832	The first book in the world to have a book jacket, *The Keepsake*, is published by Longman.
1840	The GPO issues the world's first official prepaid adhesive postage stamp, the Penny Black.
1843	Britain's first garden gnome is imported from Nuremberg by Sir Charles Isham of Lamport Hall, Northants.
1846	Ether is used as an anaesthetic for the first time in the UK, on 19 December, for a dental extraction.
1850	Elizabeth Blackwell becomes the first woman to be recognised in the UK as a qualified physician, after gaining her qualifications in America.
1851	Crystal Palace becomes the first large prefabricated building in the world.
1852	The UK's first pillarboxes are installed in Jersey, at the instigation of writer Anthony Trollope.
1863	The first underground railway in the UK opens, the Metropolitan Line from Paddington to Farringdon.
1865	Elizabeth Garrett Anderson becomes the first woman to qualify as a doctor in the UK.

LONG IN THE TOOTH

In 1816, one of Sir Isaac Newton's teeth was sold for £730 to an anonymous nobleman in London. He had the tooth set in a ring, which he then wore for the rest of his life.

HISTORIC WORDS

The Welsh are passionately devoted to their freedom and to the defence of their country. For these they fight, for these they suffer hardships. For though they, the Welsh, may be routed today, tomorrow they are ready for another campaign, quite undaunted by their losses. They are deterred by neither hunger or cold, fighting does not exhaust them nor adversity cause them despair. After an overthrow they immediately rise again ready to face the hazard of warfare once more.

Speech allegedly given by Richard I, the Lionheart

LOST OCCUPATIONS

Ale conner .... Inspector of beer and bread
Bowyer .... Maker or seller of archery bows
Broderer .... Person who embroiders
Bumbailiff .... Officer who collects debts
Cartwright .... Maker of carts
Colporteur .... Seller of books, especially bibles
Cooper .... Maker of barrels
Cordwainer .... Shoemaker, leather worker
Costermonger .... Fruit and vegetable salesman
Fletcher .... Maker of arrows
Goliard .... Wandering scholar
Gombeen man .... Irish moneylender
Horner .... Person who makes items out of horn
Scrivener .... Person who wrote out legal documents
Spelunker .... Explorer of caves
Wainwright .... Maker of carts

KEEN AS MUSTARD

The first mustard to be made in paste form rather than seed form
was sold in London in 1720 by a Mrs Clements. The jars were
covered with parchment cut from legal documents, giving rise to the
joke that deeds and contracts are 'only fit to cover mustard pots'.

THE REAL CAMELOT

One of the main claimants to the 'true' location of King Arthur's fabled Camelot is South Cadbury Hill in Somerset, a hill fort dating back to at least the pre-Roman Iron Age and occupied variously until the Saxon period. Its advocates point to its proximity to Glastonbury, which many believe was the Isle of Avalon, as well as to the recent discovery on the site of some post holes for what was once a large timber hall. This evidence further suggests that it was occupied and refortified by a post-Roman nobleman of great standing, who could possibly have been Arthur.

Local folklore includes several Arthurian legends, including the most famous – that Arthur and his knights are just sleeping below the hill, ready to awake and defend England once more when the country is in peril. But one of the main arguments for Cadbury being Camelot is that the place names fit perfectly – Queen's Camel, West Camel, the River Cam and so on. However, the flaw in the argument is that while the Somerset villages are indeed ancient, the name Camelot was invented by the French poet Chretien de Troyes in the twelfth century.

The Soldier's Song

We'll sing a song, a soldier's song,
With cheering rousing chorus,
As round our blazing fires we throng,
The starry heavens o'er us;
Impatient for the coming fight,
And as we wait the morning's light,
Here in the silence of the night,
We'll chant a soldier's song.

Chorus:
Soldiers are we whose lives are pledged to Ireland;
Some have come from a land beyond the wave.
Sworn to be free, no more our ancient sire land
Shall shelter the despot or the slave.
Tonight we man the gap of danger
In Erin's cause, come woe or weal
'Mid cannons' roar and rifles peal,
We'll chant a soldier's song.

In valley green, on towering crag,
Our fathers fought before us,
And conquered 'neath the same old flag
That's proudly floating o'er us.
We're children of a fighting race,
That never yet has known disgrace,
And as we march, the foe to face,
We'll chant a soldier's song. *[Chorus]*

Sons of the Gael! Men of the Pale!
The long watched day is breaking;
The serried ranks of Inisfail
Shall set the Tyrant quaking.
Our camp fires now are burning low;
See in the east a silv'ry glow,
Out yonder waits the Saxon foe,
So chant a soldier's song. *[Chorus]*

QUOTE UNQUOTE

*Conscription may have been good for the country,
but it damn near killed the army.*
Sir Richard Hull, British general

The first escalator in the UK was installed in Harrods department store in London, at the instigation of the manager, Richard Burbage, who disliked elevators. To soothe the nerves of first-time users, an attendant was positioned at the top to dispense brandy and sal volatile. Anyone who didn't shop at Harrods was able to try the escalator installed at Crystal Palace in south-east London, for a penny a ride.

The first escalators to be installed on the Underground were at Earls Court Station in 1911. Notices were posted warning passengers not to sit on the stairs, and to step off with the left leg first. To reassure the nervous, a man with a wooden leg known as 'Bumper' Harris was employed to ride up and down all day to demonstrate the ease and safety of the new invention. But the authorities needn't have worried; the *Illustrated London News* reported that passengers were often seen getting off a train and riding up the stairs and down again before getting back on the next train.

QUOTE UNQUOTE

When I am dead and opened, you shall find 'Calais' lying in my heart.
Queen Mary I, during whose reign Calais, England's last possession in France, was lost

DRINK TO ME ONLY

Drinks named after historic figures

Bloody Mary – vodka and tomato juice, created by Ferdinand Petiot of Harry's in New York and named after Queen Mary. It was first called Bucket of Blood, then The Red Snapper (when Worcestershire sauce, salt and pepper were added) before acquiring its royal name.

Gimlet – created by Sir TO Gimlette, British naval surgeon, who diluted his officers' gin with lime juice, believing that neat gin was harmful to the human body.

Grog – Vice Admiral Sir Edward Vernon wore a grogram coat on board ship and was known as Old Grog; when he ordered that the rum ration be watered down to reduce disorder aboard ship, the disgruntled sailors called it 'grog'.

Tom Collins – named after a nineteenth century bartender from London, who created the mixture of gin, lemon, sugar and soda water.

Rob Roy – a mixture of whisky, sweet vermouth and bitters topped with a maraschino cherry, named after the legendary Scotsman.

50 *Pounds per year paid by the Archbishop of York to lease the site of Hampton Court in 1514, on which he built a palace*

GREAT BRITISH FIRSTS: DRIVING

1862 The first traffic islands in the UK are installed in Liverpool.

1868 The first traffic lights in the UK, semaphore-style signals, are installed off Parliament Square, London.

1896 Bridget Driscoll is knocked down by a car in Crystal Palace, London, and becomes the UK's first traffic fatality.

1896 Walter Arnold becomes the first person to be convicted of speeding in the UK. He drove at 8mph past the house of a policeman in Paddock Wood, Kent, who gave chase on a bicycle and caught him red-handed. He is fined one shilling for breaking the 2mph speed limit.

1897 The first conviction for drunken driving in the UK is imposed on George Smith, who is fined 20 shillings.

1903 The first driving licence is issued in the UK for a fee of five shillings.

1903 The first car registration plates are introduced in the UK.

1926 The first pedestrian crossing in the UK is installed in Parliament Square, London.

1928 The first automatic traffic lights in the UK are installed for a one-day trial in Wolverhampton (although it was not compulsory to obey them until the 1930 Road Traffic Bill was passed).

1934 Cat's Eyes are first seen on the UK's roads.

1935 The driving test is introduced by Minister for Transport, Leslie Hore-Belisha.

1958 Parking meters are introduced in the UK, in Mayfair, London, on 10 July, costing 6d for one hour.

1960 The first fixed-penalty parking ticket in the UK is issued to Dr Thomas Creighton on 19 September. The £2 fine is waived when it is discovered that he was attending a heart-attack patient.

SUFFERING SUFFRAGETTES

Marion Wallace Dunlop, a suffragette, was the first person to go on hunger strike in Britain, after she was imprisoned for one month in 1909 for painting a clause from the Bill of Rights on the walls of the House of Commons. She was released after fasting for 91 hours. The next suffragettes who tried the same thing were force-fed until a public outcry ended the barbaric practice. However, the government then passed the Prisoners' Temporary Discharge for Ill-health Act in 1913, which was known as the Cat and Mouse Act. This meant that suffragettes were released from prison when the fasting made them ill, but were rearrested when they recovered, which was hardly an improvement. Women finally won the right to vote in 1918.

HISTORIC WORDS

Here at the world's end, on its last inch of liberty, we have lived
unmolested to this day, defended by our remoteness and obscurity...
But there are no other tribes to come; nothing but sea and cliffs and
these more deadly Romans whose arrogance you cannot escape by
obedience and self-restraint. Robbers of the world, now that the earth
falls into their all-devastating hands, they probe even the sea; if their
enemy have wealth, they have greed... neither East nor West has
glutted them... To plunder, butcher, steal, these things they misname
empire: they make a desolation and they call it peace.

**A speech allegedly made by the Caledonian general Calgacus,
after a terrible battle in 84AD between the Romans and the
'barbarians', which left 10,000 of the latter dead.**

TOO MUCH TOO YOUNG

Kings and queens of Scotland who inherited before the age of 10

Monarch	Age at accession	Year of accession
Mary Queen of Scots	7 days	1542
James VI	1 yr 36 days	1567
James V	1 yr 5 mths	1513
Margaret	2 yrs 11 mths 11 days	1286 (never crowned)
David II*	5 yrs 3 mths 2 days	1329
James II	6 yrs 4 mths 5 days	1437
Alexander III	7 yrs 10 mths 5 days	1249
James III	8 yrs 3 mths	1460

*When David II acceded to the throne at the age of five, he had
already been married for 11 months.

WHAT'S IN A NAME?

When the Angles, Jutes and Saxons swept into Britain after 450,
anyone who opposed them was shunted off into Cornwall, Wales,
Scotland and Ireland, a crescent of rebellion popularly known as
the Celtic Fringe. The Anglo-Saxons took over the rest of the
country, and referred to the rebels as 'wealisc', which means
'foreign' – and which later became, simply, 'Welsh'. The Saxons
began to refer to themselves as Angles, from which came 'Angle-
land', which became 'Engla-lond' and, finally, 'England'. But the
Scots referred to the Saxon invaders as 'Sassenach', which remains,
centuries later, a Scottish term of abuse.

OLD PICTURE, NEW CAPTION

*'What do you mean, the train hasn't been invented yet?
I've got a meeting in Guildford in an hour.'*

PAST PUZZLES

How did a king called Henry rule for 249.4 years?
Answer on page 153.

CHURCHILL AND THE
ADDISONIAN TERMINATIONS

The writer and politician Joseph Addison is perhaps best known for founding *The Spectator* in 1711, but in his day he was also notorious for ending his sentences with a preposition, a practice to which he was said to be addicted. The classical scholars of the time abhorred the behaviour, insisting that no sentence should end with a preposition. But Addison took no notice and wielded his terminations with impunity. His 'Addisonian terminations' are still frowned upon by grammatical experts, but centuries after his death, Addison found a supporter in Winston Churchill, who, when told that his sentences should not end in prepositions, retorted, firmly: 'This is a situation up with which I will not put.'

The earliest trace of human habitation in Britain was found at Boxgrove, near Chichester. The site was the camp of a group of Paleolithic hunters, and the bones were of an early species of human, *Homo heidelbergensis*, dating back 500,000 years. This is the earliest inhabitant of these islands that historians have so far been able to identify. At that time, so much of the world's water was frozen that sea level was 100 metres or more lower than it is today. This meant that Britain was joined to what is now Europe, and the first inhabitants of the British Isles probably arrived here on foot.

Over the last 700,000 years, the climate in Britain and elsewhere has gone through a process of alternating glaciation and warming; the last glaciation, or Ice Age, occurred around 13,000 years ago. It is assumed that humans came and went during this time, as the weather dictated, and that the fully modern ancestors of man, *Homo sapiens,* arrived here 30,000–40,000 years ago. A fragment of a jawbone was found in Kent's Cavern in Devon, belonging to one of these early humans. But the population only really began to grow and spread when the Mesolithic, or Middle Stone Age, period began in 10,000BC. Then, as the ice melted, the waters rose and Britain was cut off from the continent for good some time around 7,000BC. Fortunately for these early Britons,

in 8,000BC or thereabouts the climate in Britain had improved rapidly, and the island has been inhabited more or less continuously ever since.

This early Britain was probably covered with huge forests, and the hunter-gatherers who lived here would have relied on wild food, including meat – deer and wild pig – wild plants and fruit. Remains of stone axes and bows and arrows show that they perfected their hunting skills. As time passed, those living near the coast learned to enjoy seafood, while those living in areas of sandy soil created clearings that encouraged animals to gather and graze. New arrivals from the continent around 4,000–3,000BC – the beginning of the Neolithic era – brought domesticated animals as well as the technique of growing crops and of making pottery. By 3,000BC Britain was becoming a nation of farmers. The inhabitants began to build; tombs, enclosures and monuments began to shape the landscape, many of which are still standing, and towards the end of the Neolithic era more and more people were creating settlements, instead of moving around the country with the seasons. The Britons also discovered that stone and precious metals were buried in the land, and mining brought forth copper, flint, tin and iron, as well as precious stones for ornaments. Man had taken control of the land – and civilisation had begun.

A WELSH HISTORY TEST

In March 2005, *The Times* reported that the manager of the Welsh rugby team, Alan Phillips, had compiled a black book called the *Protocol Book* that he hoped would instil a sense of Welsh pride into his players. The players were expected to commit the contents to memory and were tested at random. As well as key points in Welsh history, it included famous speeches, battles, folklore and, of course, rugby history. The following facts were included:

- Llantwit Major is the oldest university town in Britain.
- Las Vegas was mostly founded by Welsh Mormons.
- The first shots in the English Civil War were fired at Pembroke Castle.
- Colonel Mainwaring, a Welshman, invented lawn tennis.
- The world's highest mountain is named after a Welshman – Sir George Everest.
- The last Briton to die in World War One was Able Seaman Richard Morgan, from Gwent.
- Jack Daniels Bourbon, Evans Williams Bourbon and Mathews Southern Comfort were all Welsh brewers who left Wales during the temperance period.
- Welshmen may have settled in America before Columbus.
- Tying a yellow ribbon around a tree was an eighteenth century Welsh tradition, practised by settlers to help other Welshmen who had travelled to a new land to find their countrymen.

QUOTE UNQUOTE

My father was frightened of his mother. I was frightened of my father and I am damned well going to see to it that my children are frightened of me.
King George V

THE HALF-HOUR WAR

The shortest British war on record took place on 27 August 1896. The British fleet, under the command of Admiral Sir Henry Rawson, turned up in Zanzibar's harbour a couple of days after Sultan Said Khaled had seized power there. The Sultan interpreted the arrival of the fleet as an act of aggression and opened fire on Rawson and his men from his only warship, the Glasgow. The considerably larger British fleet promptly fired back, destroying the Glasgow and the Sultan's palace and killing 500 of his men. The battle began at 9.12am and lasted 38 minutes.

FAMOUS LAST WORDS

The parting words of some historic figures:

I desire to leave to the men that come after me a remembrance of me in good works.
Alfred the Great, King of Wessex. Died in 899.

I will die King of England. I will not budge a foot. Treason! Treason!
King Richard III, killed at the Battle of Bosworth by Henry Tudor's troops. Died in 1485.

In vain you menace me. If all the swords in England were brandishing over my head, your terrors did not move me.
Thomas á Becket, Archbishop of Canterbury, killed in Canterbury Cathedral for challenging the authority of King Henry II. Died in 1170.

Shame, shame on a conquered king!
King Henry II, referring to the fact that his sons were conspiring against him with the King of France. Died in 1189.

The executioner is, I believe, very expert. And my neck is very slender. Oh God have pity on my soul!
Anne Boleyn, second wife of King Henry VIII. Died in 1536.

HANG ON, HELP IS ON ITS WAY

In 1705, a burglar named John Smith was hanged at Tyburn Tree. He had been suspended for a full 15 minutes when a reprieve arrived, and he was hurriedly cut down and revived. Astonishingly he survived, as the drop had not broken his neck. He was known afterwards as Half-Hanged Smith.

HISTORIC WORDS

We began our day with two large spoonfuls of sulphur and treacle. After an hour's lessons we breakfasted on one bowl of milk – 'sky-blue' we called it – and one hunk of buttered bread, unbuttered at discretion. Our dinner began with pudding, generally rice – to save the butcher's bill. As to cleanliness, I never had a bath, never bathed (at the school) during the two years I was there. On Saturday nights, before bed, our feet were washed by housemaids, in tubs around which half a dozen of us sat at a time. Woe to the last comers! For the water was never changed.

HJ Coke of Norfolk, describing his days at Temple Grove in London, one of Britain's first prep schools, established in 1810
The school's curriculum, as its founder explained, was designed that the pupils might 'daily experience those advantages which distinguish the polished gentleman from the rustic clown'.

As well as murder, execution and death in battle, Britain's monarchs found plenty of interesting ways to die, apart from old age:

Monarch	Died	Age	Cause of death
Harthacnut	1042	24	Suffered a fit; possibly poisoned
William I	1087	59	Peritonitis caused by being wounded by the pommel of his saddle
Henry I	1135	67	Ptomaine poisoning brought on by eating lampreys (eels)
Stephen	1154	57	Appendicitis
Henry II	1189	56	Haemorrhage
Richard I	1199	41	Infected arrow wound
John	1216	48	Overeating and fever led to dysentery; also possibly poisoned
Henry III	1272	65	Dementia, and grief at his brother Richard's death
Edward I	1307	68	Dysentery
Edward III	1377	64	Stroke
Henry IV	1413	45	Unknown wasting disease, possibly diabetes
Henry V	1422	34	Dysentery
Edward IV	1483	40	Overeating and indolence weakened his constitution; died of pneumonia, or typhoid
Henry VII	1509	52	Unknown. Suffered from gout and asthma
Henry VIII	1547	55	Poor health due to corpulence
Edward VI	1553	15	Tuberculosis
Mary I	1558	42	Specific cause unknown, but had congenital syphilis and influenza
Elizabeth I	1603	69	Pneumonia and severe throat infection
James I	1625	58	Gout and senility
Charles II	1685	54	Stroke
Mary II	1694	32	Smallpox
James II	1701	67	Stroke
William III	1702	51	Fell from a horse and broke his collarbone, contracted a fever, pleurisy and pneumonia
Anne	1714	49	Unknown, but was morbidly obese
George I	1727	67	Cerebral haemorrhage
George II	1760	76	Heart attack
George III	1820	81	Old age, suffered from porphyria
George IV	1830	67	Respiratory problems
William IV	1837	71	Pneumonia and cirrhosis of the liver
Victoria	1901	82	Old age
Edward VII	1910	68	Bronchial complications
George V	1936	70	Septicaemia and bronchial infection
George VI	1952	56	Lung cancer
Edward VIII	1972	77	Cancer

Number of years for which Charlotte, wife of George III, occupied the 57 throne, the longest-reigning consort in Britain

FIVE DEGREES OF NOBILITY

Britain's ranks of nobility in order of importance

Duke
Introduced to England by Edward III.
First: Edward, Prince of Wales, made Duke of Cornwall in 1337.
Title: His Grace

Marquess
Introduced to England by Richard II.
First: Robert de Vere, made Marquess of Dublin in 1385.
Title: Most Honourable

Earl
An ealdorman administered a shire or province for the king; the title became hereditary under the Normans.
First: Roger Mortimer (the first for whom the title did not derive from a county or city), made Earl of March in 1328.
Title: Right Honourable

Viscount
Once the name for a deputy or lieutenant, it was made a degree of honour by Henry VI, and viscounts were created by patent.
First: John, Lord Beaumont (first to be created by patent) made Viscount Beaumont in 1440.
Title: Right Honourable

Baron
Originally a Norman title for landowners. In the thirteenth century barons were called to parliament to represent their area, and the title became part of the peerage.
First: John de Beauchamp, (first to be created by patent, by Richard II) made Baron of Kidderminster in 1387.
Title: Right Honourable

QUOTE UNQUOTE

History, real solemn history, I cannot be interested in.... I read it a little as a duty; but it tells me nothing that does not either vex or weary me. The quarrels of popes and kings, with wars and pestilences in every page; the men all so good for nothing, and hardly any women at all.
Jane Austen, author

IN THE LINE OF DUTY

Constable William Grantham has the unfortunate distinction of being the first British policeman to be murdered while on duty. Patrolling in Somers Town in north London on 29 June 1830, the constable came across two drunken men fighting over a woman, who was watching the affray. Attempting to separate the combatants, he was knocked to the ground and kicked to death by all three.

Age of the famous fisherman Isaak Walton when he smuggled one of the crown jewels back to the exiled Charles II

LAST REQUEST

When George Bernard Shaw died in 1950, he requested in his will that his trustees commission a new 40-letter alphabet to rid the language of its difficult spellings. The alphabet was duly designed, but it failed to catch on. His only work to be published using the new alphabet was a version of *Androcles and the Lion*, published by Penguin in 1962.

LESSER-KNOWN BRITISH ECCENTRICS

William Beckford (1760–1844)

William Beckford, heir to his wealthy father's Wiltshire estate, showed great intellectual promise from an early age, taking music lessons from Mozart, learning Persian and writing Gothic novels, one of which was published when he was 21. But his promising career was cut short by rumours of a relationship with the 10-year-old Earl of Devon. Beckford became a social outcast and was denied a peerage by George III. He braved the storm for as long as he could, but eventually fled the country, supported by his £1 million inheritance.

For 13 years Beckford travelled the continent with his doctor, maître d', baker, cook, valet, three footmen and 24 musicians, who, in turn had to transport his bed, cutlery and crockery, books and prints. During a stay in Portugal, Beckford imported a flock of sheep to make the view from his window more like home, and often asked for his room to be redecorated wherever he stayed.

He eventually tired of this itinerant life and went home, where he concentrated all his energies on the building of Fonthill Abbey, which included a 300-foot octagonal tower. He supplied the builders with alcohol to ensure that they worked through the night, seven days a week, so that it would be completed as soon as possible, with the consequence that the tower fell down three times during its construction. Unable to wait, Beckford ordered that Christmas dinner be served in the abbey before the mortar was quite dry, and as the servants carried in the meal, the kitchen collapsed behind them. However, as soon as enough parts of the abbey could be persuaded to stay up, Beckford entertained the few people who would still associate with him, including Lord Nelson, and he staffed his estate with beautiful young boys. He loved animals and shared his closely guarded home with his dogs: Mrs Fry, Nephew, Tring and Viscount Fartleberry. Forced to sell the abbey in 1822, Beckford moved to Bath where he constructed another tower, this time a mere 120 feet high. He lived here until he died and the tower is now a museum dedicated to his memory. Beckford's beloved Fonthill tower, however, did not stay the course – it fell down for the last time in 1825.

TABLE MANNERS

Unacceptable behaviour at the medieval dinner table:

- Eating before everyone has been served and the lord of the manor has taken his first mouthful.
- Dipping one's bread in the soup.
- Leaving a soup spoon in the dish (it should be wiped and placed back on the table).
- Taking half-eaten food out of the mouth and putting it back on the plate.
- Dipping meat into the salt dish.
- Tipping the leftover fat from the dish on to the tablecloth.
- Licking the plate clean.
- Using a knife to pare the nails or pick the teeth.
- Wiping the knife on the tablecloth.
- Spitting on the table rather than on the ground.
- Wiping hands on the tablecloth (they should be wiped on the clothes instead).
- Using a napkin to blow one's nose.
- At the end of the meal, guests were expected to listen to grace being said, wash their hands and bow to the lord of the manor, saying 'Much good do it ye' before leaving the table.

PAST PUZZLES

Who was 'The man who lies down to shoot', 'He of the big hat' and 'The wolf who never sleeps?'
Answer on page 153.

HISTORIC WORDS

We went to Hampton Court. We walked across Bushby park, and along a raised bank beneath trees to the river. It was cold, but still. Then we took a tram to Kingston and had tea at Atkinsons, where one may have no more than a single bun. Everything is skimped now. Most of the butcher's shops are shut; the only open shop was besieged. You can't buy chocolates, or toffee; flowers cost so much I have to pick leaves instead. We have cards for most foods. The only abundant shop windows are the drapers. Other shops parade tins, or cardboard boxes, doubtless empty. (This is an attempt at the concise, historic style.) I suppose there must be some undisturbed pockets of luxury somewhere still; but the general table is pretty bare. Papers, however, flourish, and by spending sixpence we are supplied with enough to light a week's fires.

From the diary of Virginia Woolf, 5 January 1918

GREAT BRITISH FIRSTS

In 1936, 19-year-old Daphne Kearley became the UK's first air hostess. She was paid £3 a week to look after passengers on the flight from Croydon to Le Bourget. She had to be able to cook, mix cocktails, speak French, take dictation and type, as her wealthy business-class passengers would dictate letters to her en route. She also enjoyed the perk of eating first-class meals, which often included salmon and caviar. She later reported that during her first 10 months in the job, she received 299 proposals of marriage.

BRITAIN'S WORLD WAR ONE ACES

Name of pilot (* killed in action)	Type of plane flown	No. of planes shot down
Edward 'Mickey' Mannock*	SE5a	61-73
James McCudden*	SE5	54
George McElroy*	SE5a	47
Albert Ball*	Nieuports	44-47
Tom Hazell	Nieuport 17 and SE5a	43
Philip Fullard	Nieuports	40-46

THE ORIGINS OF INCOME TAX

While we accept income tax as a part of British life, it was not introduced until as late as 1799, when Pitt levied it as a way of paying for the French Revolutionary War. The rate then was two shillings in the pound. It was abolished in 1802, but quickly reinstated in 1803 by Addington, although at the lower rate of one shilling in the pound. There it remained until 1816. Then in 1842, Peel introduced a rate of seven pence in the pound for three years. Gladstone was planning to abolish it by 1860, but had his plans upset by the Crimean War, when the rate rose to one shilling and fourpence. It continued to be thought of as a temporary measure throughout Victoria's reign, and the rate remained low. Both Gladstone and Disraeli raised hopes that it might be abolished in the 1874 election – at which time the rate was only fourpence – but instead it became a relied-upon source of revenue, and has remained so ever since, with PAYE being introduced in 1944. In the first world war the rate rose to six shillings and later to ten shillings. The highest rate ever imposed on an ordinary public was 98p in the £1 in the 1970s.

*Mrs Miggins discovers that despite the end of serfdom,
she still doesn't get statutory holiday pay.*

ROYAL FLUSH

In 1953, in preparation for the coronation of Queen Elizabeth II, a number of extra toilets were installed at Westminster Abbey to save any undignified queuing on the part of the distinguished guests. But at some point before the big day, someone had a horrible thought. If all the toilets were occupied and flushed at once at a particularly solemn point in the ceremony, would the noise be captured by the BBC's sound equipment as they televised the event? The prospect was too awful to contemplate. The organisers decided that this scenario had to be tested, and a group of Guards from the nearby Wellington Barracks was summoned to the Abbey and assigned a toilet each. A number of BBC technicians were equipped with decibel meters and arranged along the line, and the order was given for all the toilets to be flushed at once. Fortunately, it was discovered that no sound could be heard inside the Abbey walls, and the nation was spared an embarrassing moment that would have become an indelible part of Britain's history.

62 *Number of Knights of the Garter created by James I on his coronation day, 25 July 1603*

HOW ENGLISH IS ENGLISH?

The many occupiers of the British Isles, and forays into other lands by British explorers have ensured that the Queen's English has a very mixed bag of origins indeed. Here is a handful of the most well-known 'borrowings' from places around the world:

The Americas:
anorak, barbecue, buccaneer, cannibal, chilli, chocolate, hammock, hurricane, parka, pecan, poncho, potato, tobacco, toboggan, tomato

Africa:
banjo, commando, jazz, juke (box), mumbo-jumbo, raffia, trek, voodoo, zombie

Asia (western):
admiral, alchemy, alcohol, algebra, almanac, alphabet, arsenal, assassin, behemoth, caravan, checkmate, cherub, coffee, divan, hallelujah, hazard, horde, kiosk, lemon, leviathan, magazine, magic, mammoth, mogul, paradise, pyjamas, sequin, sofa, spinach, syrup, tariff, tiara, tulip, turkey, zenith, zero

Southern and south-eastern Asia:
bungalow, caddy, chintz, chutney, compound, crimson, dinghy, dungaree, gingham, guru, gymkhana, juggernaut, jungle, junk, lacquer, loot, mandarin, mantra, pariah, pundit, sapphire, shampoo, sugar, swastika

Central and eastern Asia:
china, chin-chin, gung-ho, judo, kamikaze, ketchup, kowtow, tea, tycoon

Europe (Germanic):
anger, balderdash, bluff, blunder, boss, bully, bumpkin, coleslaw, cookie, dapper, doze, egg, fellow, flimsy, frolic, golf, grime, hamster, inkling, loiter, muck, nasty, nudge, oaf, poppycock, rant, scowl, smack, smuggle, spook, ugly, window, yacht

Europe (Greek):
agnostic, analyst, antithesis, automaton, biology, blasphemy, charisma, cinema, crisis, criterion, critic, diagnosis, dinosaur, dogma, drama, electron, enigmatic, genesis, hoi polloi, patriarch, phenomenon, photograph, stigma, synthesis

Europe (Latin):
apex, area, bacteria, camera, circus, complex, equilibrium, formula, fungus, genius, inertia, interim, medium, momentum, opera, pauper, pendulum, propaganda, referen-dum, series, simile, status, vertigo, victor

Europe (Romance languages):
anchovy, barricade, battalion, beauty, brochure, camouflage, castle, charlatan, chivalry, conquest, defeat, design, dessert, dinner, embargo, garage, garden, honest, loyal, morale, mutton, nutmeg, palaver, paste, poison, prestige, quest, royal, souvenir, tempest, ticket

A1 DRIVER

When registration plates were introduced in Britain in 1903, the much-coveted A1 number plate was secured by the 2nd Earl Russell for his 12 hp Napier. The plate was bequeathed to a Trevor Laker of Leicester in 1950 and sold in August 1959 for £2,500, which was given to charity.

HOW FAR IS THAT IN NAILS?

Imperial measures of distance:
1 mile = 1,760 yards
1 furlong = 220 yards
1 cable = 600 feet
1 chain = 22 yards = 100 links
1 rod, pole or perch = 5 1/2 yards
1 fathom = 6 feet
1 yard = 3 feet = 36 inches
1 foot = 12 inches
1 span = 9 inches
1 hand = 4 inches
1 nail = 2 1/4 inches (for cloth)
1 inch = 1/36 of a yard

FAMOUS LAST WORDS

The parting words of some historic figures:

By the Immortal God, I will not move.
Thomas Love Peacock, writer, who burned to death in 1866 trying to save his beloved library of books.

Oh, I am so bored with it all.
Winston Churchill, prime minister. Died 1965.

When I am dead, I hope it may be said, His sins were scarlet, but his books were read.
Epitaph written for himself by **Hilaire Belloc**, though not inscribed on his tombstone. Died 1953.

I realise that patriotism is not enough. I must have no hatred or bitterness towards anyone.
Edith Cavell, nurse, executed by a German firing squad in 1915.

I am going outside and may be some time.
Captain Lawrence Oates, as he sacrificed his own life in 1912 to save those of his fellow explorers on their ill-fated Antarctic expedition.

So little done. So much to do!
Alexander Graham Bell, inventor of the telephone. Died in 1922.

To begin with, the government left moral supervision to voluntary and philanthropic organizations, who were quickly alerted to the 'grave moral dangers' threatened by war, especially to young women. While recruits had been sent to war armed with a personal exhortation from Lord Kitchener to exercise self-control and guard against temptation, women's duty, the Bishop of London warned, was 'to send out the young man in the right spirit, free from moral stain'. This was rapidly deemed inadequate by vigilance organizations. According to the National Union of Women Workers, 'the girlhood of the country was thrown off its balance' by the excitement of war; large numbers of khaki-clad men had 'excited its imagination and aroused its patriotism', and this was 'unfortunately...expressed by foolish, giddy, irresponsible conduct'. The NUWW at once realized that girls' behaviour 'might result in leading them into grave moral danger; and it determined to try to save them from their own folly.'

The remedy was to set up part-time voluntary women's patrols 'to befriend and guide young girls'. Patrols became a semi-official branch of the government's policing efforts, when the Home Secretary and most police authorities granted them official recognition and authorized their activities. By 1917, 2,284 patrols, some paid out of police funds, were patrolling parks, open spaces, railway stations and streets, not only befriending 'foolish girls and saving them from danger, and warning girls who behave unsuitably', but also saving men from 'women of evil reputation' as well as sorting out drunken soldiers 'by means of cups of black coffee laced with bicarbonate of soda which, after making them violently sick, left them sober enough to be entrained in due course'.

Regular liaison was maintained with police and military authorities. For instance, when the army claimed young girls were using the excuse of collecting soldier's washing to hang around billets, patrols ensured that only men or boys carried out this duty and reported any woman doing it. They had seats used by couples for amorous purposes boarded up. One intrepid patrol watching a towpath in the depths of winter was 'astonished to find soldiers and girls sitting on seats far up the river on the terribly cold nights. Apart from the moral danger, the danger of falling into the river was great. Another seemed surprised that 'daylight and people about seem not to matter in the least. You come on a heaped mass of arms and legs and much stocking and they are too absorbed to know we are there.'

Cate Haste,
Rules of Desire: Sex in Britain, World War One to the Present
Social historian, explains the government's attempts to restrain the nation's youth as WWI began to loosen their morals.

FAMOUS HISTORIC DOGS

Dog	Owner
Boatswain	Lord Byron
Bounce	Alexander Pope
Boy	Prince Rupert
Cabal	King Arthur
Dash	Charles Lamb
Diamond	Isaac Newton
Flush	Elizabeth Barratt Browning
Geist, Kaiser	Matthew Arnold
Hamlet, Maida	Sir Walter Scott
Mathe	Richard II
Rufus	Winston Churchill

GREAT BRITONS

Boudicca, Queen of the Iceni (died 61AD)

Boudicca was the wife of Prasutagus, the king of the Iceni at the time of the Roman invasion of 43AD. As Prasutagus thrived in the years following the invasion, it is assumed that he had agreed to negotiate with the Romans, as many leaders did, to avoid slavery or annihilation. He bequeathed half his kingdom to the Romans, and the other half to his teenage daughters, an arrangement that Boudicca was content to abide by. However, when the King died, Nero declared the area a slave province, a punishment more usually meted out to those who resisted Roman rule. The Romans began pillaging the kingdom, and when Boudicca protested, she was flogged and her daughters raped. It was a huge mistake on the Romans' part; Boudicca became their worst enemy, and many Britons were so incensed at her treatment that they rose in revolt.

In 61AD the Iceni and the Trinovantes joined forces to destroy first the town of Colchester, a Roman city, and then London. No one was spared; Britons and Romans alike were burned and slaughtered as Boudicca tried to rid the country of both invaders and traitors. The rebels then turned on St Albans, where the Catuvellauni had made peace with the Romans. As battle commenced, it seemed the Britons must win; they vastly outnumbered the Romans and were brave and fierce. But they were also disorganised, which the Romans were not, and the Britons were defeated, with losses of up to 80,000. Boudicca survived, but rather than fall into the hands of the Romans, she took poison and persuaded her daughters to do the same. Although her rebellion failed, she survives in British history as a symbol of courage and patriotism.

At first, many were fooled by the French army's inflatable decoys.

HISTORIC WORDS

For eight years I have struggled with much labour for my right to the kingdom and for honourable liberty. I have lost brothers, friends and kinsmen. Your own kinsmen have been made captive and bishops and priests are locked in prison. Our nobility's blood has poured forth in war. Those barons you can see before you, clad in mail, are bent on destroying me and obliterating my kingdom, nay our whole nation. They do not believe we can survive. They glory in their war-horses and equipment. For us the name of the Lord must be our hope of victory in battle. This is a day of rejoicing; the birthday of John the Baptist. With our Lord Jesus as commander, Saint Andrew and the martyr Saint Thomas shall fight to day with the saints of Scotland for the honour of their country and their nation. If you heartily repent for your sins you will be victorious under God's command.

The words of Robert the Bruce to his troops, as they faced Edward II's army at Bannockburn in June 1314
The Scots were victorious, but the battle between England and Scotland continued for centuries to come.

MUSIC FOR THE MONARCH

Masters of the King's (or Queen's) Music:

1625	Nicholas Lanier	1834	Christian Kramer
1666	Louis Grabu	1848	George F Anderson
1674	Nicholas Staggins	1870	William George Cusins
1700	John Eccles	1893	Walter Parratt
1735	Maurice Greene	1924	Edward Elgar
1755	William Boyce	1934	Walford Davies
1779	John Stanley	1942	Arnold Bax
1786	William Parsons	1953	Arthur Bliss
1817	William Shield	1975	Malcolm Williamson

PAST PUZZLES

Why was the Korean War bad for British teeth?
Answer on page 153.

Answer on page 153.

WITCHES, PROPHETS AND MYSTIC MEN

John Dee

Born in Wales in 1527, John Dee was the son of a court official. Educated at the new Cambridge University, he proved to be so clever that he was considered to be one of England's most learned men. So learned, in fact, that many thought him to be a wizard.

At the time, the country was in the hands of Queen Mary, who was busy expunging the nation of Protestants. Many would have preferred her half-sister, Elizabeth, to be on the throne, and Elizabeth lived in constant fear of her life. Fearing the worst, Robert Dudley, a supporter and suitor of Elizabeth, went to Dee to ask for his advice. Dee drew up the young woman's horoscope, and predicted that she would not, in fact, be beheaded by Mary as she feared, but would become queen. When Mary heard of the prophesy, she had Dee thrown into the Tower, along with Elizabeth and Dudley. Fortunately they escaped execution and when Mary died in 1558, leaving the throne free for Elizabeth, Dee's fortunes were restored and he was made Astrologer Royal. He chose a propitious date for Elizabeth's coronation and continued to advise the Queen, throughout her reign. In 1583, he predicted 'the appearing of the very great sea and many ships thereon', at which the queen ordered more ships to be built. When the Spanish Armada appeared off England's shores five years later, England was ready for them. Sadly, Dee also predicted the one thing that the Queen would not change; that she would neither marry nor produce an heir.

INFLATED VALUES

On 22 April 1659, the first cheque to be drawn on a British bank was made out to the bearer by one Nicholas Vanacker, for the sum of £10. The original cheque was sold at Sotheby's for £1,300 in 1976.

FAST FOOD

Price list from a cookshop in London in 1378, for ready-to-eat roasted food:

Heron	18d
Bittern	18d
Pheasant	13d
Capon baked in pastry	8d
Lamb	7d
Baked capon (no pastry)	6d
Rabbit	4d
Plover, woodstock, teal	2 1/2d
Thrushes	2d for 3
Finches	1d for 10

QUOTE UNQUOTE

Remember that you are an Englishman, and have consequently won first prize in the lottery of life.
Cecil Rhodes, founder of the state of Rhodesia

SEXUAL PENALTIES

During his reign, King Canute attempted to change the rather casual Anglo-Saxon attitude to sex and marriage by introducing a law that if a woman committed adultery, she lost all her property to her husband and had her nose and ears cut off. Fortunately, his draconian law died with him. However, during the Dark Ages there was an interesting selection of fines available for cases of sexual misconduct or assault:

- For lying with a virgin who was merely a slave: 12 shillings
- For lying with a virgin who worked in the royal flour mill: 25 shillings (for reasons of hygiene, perhaps)
- For lying with a virgin who was a servant in the royal household: 50 shillings
- For fondling the breast of a woman without consent: 5 shillings
- For throwing a woman to the floor: 10 shillings
- For rape: 60 shillings (paid to the woman herself)

FIRST BRITISH DAILY NEWSPAPERS

Daily Courant	1702	London (first successful daily)
Belfast News Letter	1737	Belfast
The Press and Journal	1748	Aberdeen
The Herald	1783	Glasgow
The Times	1785	London
The Observer	1791	London
The Courier	1816	Dundee
The Scotsman	1817	Edinburgh
The Guardian	1821	London
Evening Standard	1827	London

LONELY HEARTS CLUB

When a spinster named Helen Morison became the first person in Britain to advertise for a husband, by placing a notice in the *Manchester Weekly Journal* in 1727, there was such outrage at her immorality that the Lord Mayor had Miss Morison committed to a lunatic asylum for four weeks.

THE SOMERSET TSUNAMI

In 1607, an enormous wave roared up the Bristol Channel and burst over the coast of Somerset, sweeping away villages, bridges, people and livestock. The wave flooded hundreds of square miles of land, drowned 2000 people and was seized upon by religious pamphleteers as an opportunity to warn against invoking the wrath of God. William Jones in his pamphlet *God's Warning to his People of England* claimed that the flood was the third of three dire warnings to England, preceded by the 1603 plague and the Gunpowder Plot. 'Many are the dombe warnings of destruction, which the Almighty God hath lately scourged this our kingdome with... all which, in bleeding hearts, may inforce us to put on the true garment of repentance,' he warned. The *Lamentable Newes* pamphlet agreed, laying the blame on idle gentry and clergy. 'The Cleargie doth nothing but looke for livings, and leave the labours of their function; and the Gentry esteeme more of their Hawkes, Houndes, and other their vainer pleasures then the godly discharging of their offices wherein the Lord hath set them,' it fumed. The catastrophe was a chance for the Puritans to vent their fury at attempts to relax anti-Catholic legislation and at the dismissal of Puritan clergy. But while their anger may have been justified, it was of little use to ordinary citizens, who had to wait a full 10 days before the waters receded and life could begin again.

---

70 *Number of inhabitants in London, in thousands, thought to have been slaughtered by Boadicea and the Iceni in 60AD*

TWENTIETH-CENTURY CRISES

The Suez Crisis (1956)

In 1956, the Suez Canal Company was largely controlled by the British government, and the canal itself was of huge strategic importance. The French had the next biggest stake. An agreement signed in 1888 gave the Suez Canal Company concessionary rights to the use of the canal until 1968. However, in July 1956, President Nassar of Egypt nationalised the Canal Company, in order to use the shipping tolls to build the Aswan High Dam. The British government, led by Anthony Eden, secretly resolved to bring down the Egyptian government, and the British, French and Israeli governments hatched a plan in which Israel would attack Egypt, and the British and French would come in to mediate and regain control of the canal. The Israeli invasion went ahead on 29 October, followed by the British and French landing on 5 November, which set off an international uproar. All three countries were forced to withdraw and were replaced by a UN peacekeeping force. Anthony Eden resigned in January 1957 on the grounds of ill-health.

QUOTE UNQUOTE

*Get rid of the lunatic who says he's got
a machine for seeing by wireless.*
The editor of the *Daily Express*, referring to John Logie Baird

THE DUTIES OF A SHERIFF

- To superintend revictualment of the castle
- To provide funds for the siege of the castle
- To expel intruders into manors and to arrest rebels with *posse comitatus* (ie using citizens rather than soldiers)
- To maintain the peace of the realm with *posse comitatus*
- To summon 12 men of the county to attend to justice
- To enquire into the capture of King's officers by rebels
- To grant administration of estates
- To enforce observation of the great charter
- To summon complainants to the King's court
- To send revenues of counties, hundreds and demesnes to the King
- To summon tenants in chief, burgesses and knights of the shire before justices of the eyre
- To send knights to confer with the King
- To elect coroners
- To attend the King

Before the Wars of the Roses began in 1455, the rivalry between the houses of Lancaster and York was already sorely felt. The reigning king, the Lancastrian Henry VI, had surrounded himself with unpopular noblemen, and when he fell ill in 1454, his second cousin, Richard, Duke of York, was appointed Protector of the Realm. He set about clearing out Henry's advisors, but when the King recovered, he dismissed the Duke's protection. Richard then challenged him to the first battle of the Wars of the Roses at St Albans. Henry was defeated and seemed willing to be reconciled. But when he fell ill again, Richard once more became protector, only to be dismissed again a year later and the whole thing started again.

Henry's wife, Margaret, despised Richard and encouraged her allies to rise against him. Soon the country was divided and the Wars began in earnest at the battle of Ludlow in 1459. Over the next decade war raged, victory followed defeat and sides were swopped. In 1460, Parliament named Richard as heir instead of Henry's son, Edward. Henry agreed, but Margaret raised an army to fight the Yorkists at Wakefield and Richard was killed.

The Yorkists swiftly raised another army, declaring Richard's son (also called Edward) to be the king. The Lancastrians were defeated at Towton, Richard's son was crowned King Edward IV in 1461 and Henry was banished to the Tower of London.

But it didn't end there. In October 1470, after another encounter saw King Edward flee the country, Henry was reinstated as King for a few months. But in 1471 Edward returned to London with an army to reclaim his title, and Henry's son was killed in battle at Tewkesbury a month later. Margaret was imprisoned and Henry was stabbed to death in the Tower, although it was passed off as a 'natural' death, to prevent any rebellions.

But still the Wars went on. In 1485, trouble flared up once more, although this time it was York against York. When Edward IV died, his 12-year-old son, Edward V, fell under the protection of his Uncle Richard, Edward IV's brother. Confining the young King and his brother to the Tower, Richard claimed that Edward IV's marriage had been invalid, and that the boys were illegitimate. Parliament agreed, and Richard was proclaimed King. The boys conveniently disappeared, and it is assumed they were murdered by the new king.

But Richard III had a problem in the form of the last remaining Lancastrian claimant, Henry Tudor, who was biding his time in Brittany. In 1485, Henry confronted Richard's forces at the Battle of Bosworth. Richard was killed and Henry claimed the crown. Apart from a scuffle at Stoke in 1487, when Lambert Simnel tried to become King by pretending to be a suitable heir, the Wars of the Roses were over.

72 *Height in feet of the east window in Gloucester Cathedral, commemorating the Battle of Crecy*

COULD THIS BE AVALON?

Legend has it that Glastonbury Tor in Somerset is the burial place of King Arthur, the real Isle of Avalon. The problem with this theory is that, in the story, the Isle of Avalon keeps appearing and then disappearing, whereas Glastonbury Tor sticks out like a sore thumb from the surrounding countryside, and only ever disappears once a year under a swarm of new age festival-goers.

But it wasn't always so. Until the late eighteenth century, when the Great Drains began to be built, the Somerset Levels were tidal, and many hills, including Glastonbury Tor, were a place of safety until the floods receded with the tide. And thus, at certain times the 'Island of Glastonbury' could indeed be said to have appeared and then disappeared again.

HISTORIC WORDS

Carriages without horses shall go,
And accidents fill the world with woe,
Around the Earth thoughts shall fly,
In the twinkling of an eye.

Through the hills man shall ride,
And no horse be at his side.
Under water men shall walk,
Shall ride, shall sleep, shall talk,
In the air men shall be seen,
In white in black in green.
Iron on the water will float
As easily as a wooden boat.

Fire and water shall wonders do
England shall at last admit a foe
The world to an end shall come
In eighteen hundred and eighty-one.

Although first thought to be the work of legendary prophet Mother Shipton, this verse was in fact written by Charles Hindley in 1862, who later admitted it was a forgery.
According to the few facts that can be discerned, there was a woman named Mother Shipton who lived in a cave in Yorkshire. She predicted a number of major historic events, including King Henry's six wives and the fall of Cardinal Wolsey. Despite arousing the wrath of the King she was never accused of witchcraft and died peacefully in 1561. Mother Shipton's Cave, in Knaresborough is now a tourist attraction.

TRIBES OF ROMAN BRITAIN

In the late first century BC, tribes were emerging all over Britain, as the people settled and began to establish communities. In the first century AD, the tribes comprised the following:

Atrebates • Boresti • Brigantes • Caledonii
Careni • Carnonacae • Cantiaci • Carvetii
Catuvellauni • Coritani • Cornavii • Cornovii
Creones • Decantae • Deceangli • Demetae
Dobunni • Dumnonii • Durotriges • Epidii
Iceni • Lugi • Novantae • Ordovices • Parisi
Selgovae • Silures • Smertae • Taexali
Trinovantes • Vacomagii • Venicones • Votadini

HISTORIC WORDS

Anthem for Doomed Youth

What passing-bells for these who die as cattle?
Only the monstrous anger of the guns.
Only the stuttering rifles' rapid rattle
Can patter out their hasty orisons.
No mockeries now for them; no prayers nor bells,
Nor any voice of mourning save the choirs, -
The shrill, demented choirs of wailing shells;
And bugles calling for them from sad shires.

What candles may be held to speed them all?
Not in the hands of boys, but in their eyes
Shall shine the holy glimmers of good-byes.
The pallor of girls' brows shall be their pall;
Their flowers the tenderness of patient minds,
And each slow dusk a drawing down of blinds.

Wilfred Owen, Anthem for Doomed Youth
The poet was killed in action a week before the Armistice ended World War One.

IT COULD BE YOU

Britain's first National Lottery was launched in 1567 to pay for a variety of public works. The tickets cost 10 shillings each, of which 400,000 were sold and the first prize was £5,000, although only £3,000 was paid in cash; the rest was paid in a variety of goods, such as cloth, tapestry and plate. It was a one-off event and was very successful, but was not repeated until the following century, and did not become a weekly fixture until over 400 years later.

King Alfred the Great (847-899)

Alfred was the only English king to be called 'the Great'. But what made him so great?

In 871, Alfred became King of Wessex, one of the country's seven kingdoms. The lack of unity made the country vulnerable to invaders, and when the Vikings arrived in 793, there was no single army to stand against them. And so, they waged war across the country for nearly three hundred years, until the beginning of the Norman reign.

Amidst this confusion came Alfred. With his elder brother, King Ethelred of Wessex, he trounced the Vikings at the Battle of Ashdown in 870. However, the brothers were defeated in subsequent battles and Ethelred died of his wounds in 871. Now King, Alfred managed to restore peace that same year, but when trouble flared again a few years later, he was forced to take refuge in Somerset. There he raised an army and returned to defeat the invaders at Edington in Wiltshire in 878. It was this that saved England from total Danish conquest. In a settlement with the Vikings, he divided England along Watling Street, a Roman road that cut diagonally across the country from Dover to Chester. He confined the Vikings to the east of this road, where they established the Danelaw.

Alfred then designed a number of reforms that would make him better prepared for future invasions. He arranged that half of the fyrd (land-workers who joined the army when needed) would work on the land, and the other half would be always on active military service. The two halves swopped at regular intervals, so both could keep their hand in. Alfred's thegns (the highest order of a Saxon household) also served the King for one month out of three. He also set up a system of fortified burghs, which served as assembly points for the fyrd. They were situated so no man would be more than a day's march from a fortress. He also built a fleet that defeated an invasion of Vikings in 897, and he is often referred to as the father of the Navy.

Alfred's greatness was not only military. He translated important religious texts into English and designed candles that would tell the time. He wrote laws and saw that they were kept. He encouraged education, the restoration of monasteries and – from 889 – the writing of the *Anglo-Saxon Chronicles*. He died in 899, leaving a better country in the hands of his son, Edward.

Although Alfred is often referred to as the first king of England, it was Edward who drove the Danes out of the east and was first to rule all of England south of the Humber. His son, Athelstan, added Northumbria to the kingdom. But perhaps because of Alfred's vision of a united England and the vital work he did that helped his descendants to realise that aim, he is popularly thought of as our first king.

OLD PICTURE, NEW CAPTION

Charles realised that he had long overlooked the benefits of allowing women to join his gentleman's club.

QUOTE UNQUOTE

Great Britain has lost an Empire and has not yet found a role.
Dean Acheson, US Secretary of State, 1949-1952

PECULIAR PATRON SAINTS

St George of England was not English. He was probably Greek or Turkish, although his provenance has never been fully established.

St Patrick of Ireland was born at 'Bannavem Taberniae', part of Roman Britain, which we know from his own writings. This has been identified with many places, including Carlisle, Devon and Wales, but not anywhere in Ireland.

St Andrew of Scotland was one of Jesus's 12 disciples, which qualifies him for sainthood, but means he almost certainly wasn't Scottish.

St David of Wales was in fact the only native of the country for which he is a patron saint.

SPEAKING OF THE DEAD

Obituary notices from British history

Exit Burbage.
Alleged epitaph for **Richard Burbage**, Shakespearean actor. Died in 1619.

Nature and Nature's laws lay hid in night:
God said, 'Let Newton be!' and there was light.
Epitaph for **Sir Isaac Newton**, written by Alexander Pope. Died in 1727.

George IV contributed more to the demoralization of society than any prince recorded in the pages of history.
Comment by biographer Robert Huish, on the death of **King George IV**. Died in 1830.

There never was an individual less regretted by his fellow creatures than this deceased King. What heart has heaved one sob of unnecessary sorrow?
The Times obituary for **King George IV**. Died in 1830.

Aden, Monday – Dr Livingstone died in June, of dysentery, at Lake Bembe, after wading through water for four days. His body has been preserved in salt by his native servants, and is proceeding to Zanzibar.
Telegram reporting the death of the explorer **Dr David Livingstone**. Died in 1873.

An honest, faithful and devoted follower, a trustworthy, discreet, and straightforward man, and possessed of strong sense; he filled a position of great and anxious responsibility, the duties of which he performed with such constant and unceasing care as to secure for himself the real friendship of the Queen.
The death of **John Brown**, devoted manservant of Queen Victoria, as reported in the *Official Court Circular*. Died in 1883.

I've just read that I am dead. Don't forget to delete me from your list of subscribers.
Rudyard Kipling, on reading his premature obituary. Died in 1936.

Here lies Robert Maxwell. He lies everywhere else.
Obituary in *Private Eye* on the media mogul, who was frequently mocked, castigated and scorned by the magazine, an attitude fully justified by **Robert Maxwell**'s shameful misappropriation of employee pension funds. Died in 1991.

Dressed in howlingly unfashionable clothes and armed with a rusty bullhorn, he campaigned in more than 40 elections, losing them all but winning for himself the appreciation of a society with a fondness for eccentrics.
Obituary of **David 'Screaming' Lord Sutch**, leader of the Official Monster Raving Loony Party. Died in 1999.

GREAT BRITISH FIRSTS

1843	First paid telegrams in the UK are sent, costing 1 shilling.
1864	First Christmas Day swim in the Serpentine in Hyde Park, London, takes place.
1875	Captain Matthew Webb becomes the first man to swim the Channel, reaching France in 21 hours and 45 minutes (he died in 1883 trying to swim the Niagara Falls).
1880	First telephone directory in the UK is published.
1881	First electric power station to provide electricity for public and domestic use: Central Power Station, Godalming, Surrey.
1887	First women's cricket club is formed in Yorkshire, the White Heather Club.
1887	The first photographically illustrated advertisement is published in *The Parrot* by the Harrison Patent Knitting Machine Company.
1896	The Duchesse de Clermont-Tonnerre is the first woman to smoke in public in the UK, in the dining room of the Savoy Hotel, London.

PAST PUZZLES

Who was the last English king to die in battle?
Answer on page 153.

NINE TO FIVE

The alternative careers of some historic figures

Joseph Addison, *writer* . . . . MP for Malmesbury
Clement Attlee, *prime minister* . . . . social worker
Alexander Graham Bell, *inventor* . . . . . . speech teacher to the deaf
Arnold Bennett, *writer* . . . . solicitor's clerk
Daniel Defoe, *writer* . . . . brickmaker and shopkeeper
Benjamin Disraeli, *prime minister* . . . . novelist
John Donne, *poet* . . . . Dean of St Paul's
Michael Faraday, *scientist* . . . . bookseller and laboratory
bottle-washer
Edward Gibbon, *historian* . . . . MP for Liskeard
Gerard Manley Hopkins, *poet* . . . . classics professor
Harold Macmillan, *prime minister* . . . . publisher
Isaac Newton, *scientist* . . . . Master of the Royal Mint
and Member for Parliament
George Orwell, *writer* policeman
Walter Raleigh, *explorer* . . . . MP for Devon
Laurence Sterne, *writer* . . . . vicar
Edmund Hillary, *mountaineer* . . . . beekeeper

HISTORIC WORDS

In England, following the restoration of a monarchy subject to parliamentary authority, pre-publication censorship was abolished, in 1695, opening up a period in which British journalism blossomed, nurturing talents as diverse as those of Daniel Defoe, Joseph Addison, Richard Steele, Jonathan Swift, John Wilkes and Thomas Paine. As journalism expanded on many fronts, it began to encounter notions of journalistic ethics and professional practice...

Journalism, already in tension with itself about its methods, would be engulfed in battle with the state. Having abandoned the weapon of direct, pre-publication censorship, the British government turned to taxation, in the form of a stamp duty, designed to prevent newspapers becoming too popular and to mark out the respectable from the unrespectable. A more blatant technique was to pay journalists retainers in order to induce them to write more favourable copy. Meanwhile, the libel laws evolved to punish newspapers guilty of defamation or, occasionally, the more serious criminal offence of seditious libel.

In this nascent democracy, the press acquired a unique position, locating itself physically in Fleet Street, between London's business district to the east and Parliament to the west. When the press found itself in conflict with the authorities, it would then, as now, appeal to public opinion or, in the language of the time, 'the London mob'. Large sections of the early press were umbilically tied to the aspirations of their readers for a more democratic society.

Ian Hargreaves, documenting the first reporters in *Journalism: Truth or Dare?*

HOME FROM HOME

The word 'Blighty', first used by British soldiers stationed in India to refer fondly to home, is a corruption of a Hindustani word bilayati, which means 'foreign country'.

SHORTEST PEERAGE

The shortest peerage in Britain lasted a split second, due to a legal technicality. The law assumed that the Hon Wilfrid Carlyl Stamp, the second Baron Stamp, survived his father by a split second on 16 April 1941, when he and the first Baron Stamp were both killed in an air raid. The shortest recorded peerage apart from this unlikely event was that of 30 minutes; 13-year-old Charles Brandon, third Duke of Suffolk, died 30 minutes after succeeding his elder brother, Henry, when both were felled by a fatal illness on 14 July 1551.

NAMED AND FAMED

Well-known nouns and the people who inspired them

Bobby/Peeler Sir Robert Peel (1788-1850), prime minister, set up the first police force.

Boycott Captain Charles Boycott (1832-1897) collected rents for Lord Earne from Irish tenant farmers. When he refused their request for rent cuts, Charles Parnell called for everyone to suspend dealings with Boycott. It proved highly successful.

Cardigan The seventh Earl of Cardigan (1797-1868), leader of the Charge of the Light Brigade, wore a knitted worsted jacket, which evolved into the modern cardigan.

Derby Edward Smith-Stanley (1752-1834), twelfth Earl of Derby, established the Epsom Derby in 1780.

Derrick Goodman Derick, seventeenth-century hangman, inspired the term for this hoisting crane.

Farad Michael Faraday (1791-1867) made the first electrical transformer; this unit of electrical capacitance is named after him.

Macintosh Charles Macintosh (1766-1843), patented the waterproof coat in 1823.

Kelvin William Thomson, Lord Kelvin (1824-1907), gave his name to this unit of temperature.

Newton Sir Isaac Newton (1642-1727), discoverer of gravity, gave his name to this unit of force.

Sandwich John Montagu, the fourth Earl of Sandwich (1718-1792), was a compulsive gambler and had his food brought to the card table, pressed between two slices of bread.

Shrapnel Henry Shrapnel (1761-1842), English artillery officer, invented the fragmenting explosive.

THE ENDLESS PARLIAMENT

The longest English parliament... lasted for 17 years, eight months and 16 days. It was known as the 'Pensioners' Parliament' and took place during the reign of Charles II, from 8 May 1661 to 24 January 1679.

The longest United Kingdom parliament... was during the reign of George V, Edward VIII and George VI, lasting an unbroken nine years, six months and 20 days, from 26 November 1935 to 15 June 1945.

The shortest parliament... was that of Edward I, which lasted only one day, 30 May 1306.

---

80 *Age of Thomas Parr, England's oldest man, when he married for the first in time 1563 (after which he had an affair, which resulted in a love-child)*

QUOTE UNQUOTE

History. An account, mostly false, of events, mostly unimportant, which are brought about by rulers, mostly knaves, and soldiers, mostly fools.
Ambrose Bierce, *The Devil's Dictionary*

TEN VICTIMS OF JACK THE RIPPER

Emma Elizabeth Smith	died 3 April 1888	*aged 45*
Martha Turner	died 7 August 1888	*aged 35*
Mary Ann Nicholls	died 31 August 1888	*aged 42*
Annie Chapman	died 8 September 1888	*aged 47*
Elizabeth Stride	died 30 September 1888	*aged 45*
Catherine Eddowes	died 30 September 1888	*aged 43*
Mary Jane Kelly	died 9 November 1888	*aged 24*
Elizabeth Jackson	died June 1889	*age unknown*
Alice Mackenzie	died 17 July 1889	*aged 47*
Frances Coles	died 13 February 1891	*aged 25*

WITCHES, PROPHETS AND MYSTIC MEN

Coinneach Odhar

Coinneach Odhar, a one-eyed Scotsman, lived in the Hebrides in the seventeenth century, and was known for his predictions of the future, earning himself the nickname 'The Brahan Seer'. Odhar would stare through a hole in a pebble with his good eye and claim to 'see' the future. He foresaw the invention of the train, the construction of the Caledonian Canal in 1822, the invention of gas lighting and piped water and the Battle of Culloden. 'The bleak moor shall, ere many generations have passed away, be stained with the best blood of the Highlands,' he claimed. 'Glad am I that I will not see that day, for it will be a fearful period, heads will be lopped off by the score, and no mercy will be shown or quarter given on either side.' The battle, in 1746, was indeed ferocious and bloody, with thousands of Scotsmen killed. Odhar later sealed his own fate by telling his employer, Lady Seaforth, that her husband was dallying with another woman overseas; furious, she condemned him to a horrible death, but not before he made his last prediction, which foresaw the end of the Seaforth line. He predicted that a deaf and dumb man would be predeceased by all his four sons and the estate would pass to a woman, who would kill her sister. All of it came true; when the last Seaforth died in 1815, after his four sons, the estate passed to the eldest daughter, who accidentally killed her sister in 1823 while driving a carriage.

GREAT BRITONS

Clive of India (1725-1774)

Robert Clive was born in Shropshire in 1725. At the age of 18, he obtained a clerkship with the East India Company in Madras, which, two years later, was captured by the French. Clive was taken prisoner but escaped and in 1747 was commissioned as an Ensign in the East India Company's army. Despite having had no formal military training, he proved to be a natural soldier and was rapidly promoted after leading the company's troops in several engagements, achieving dazzling victories in every case.

At Arcot, capital of the Carnatic, on 31 August 1755, as a mere Captain, he led 200 men from the first Madras European Regiment and 300 sepoys, and captured and occupied the half-ruined fort. There, he resisted a siege of 50 days and finally beat off the attacking force of 10,000 trained troops of the Nawab and 300 Frenchmen.

His greatest success was at Plassey on the 23 June 1757 where with 300 men of the 39th Foot (later the Dorsetshire Regiment – the first English regiment to serve in India) 750 Madras Europeans and 1500 Indian troops he defeated the 50,000 strong army of the Nawab of Bengal and established British supremacy there, as he had done at Arcot in Madras.

However, the climate and strains of combat took their toll and he was invalided home, only to find himself a national hero. He made – and quickly spent – a fortune, and returned to India in 1755, where he was appointed Governor of Bengal in 1757. When he returned to England a few years later, he was elected MP for Shrewsbury and created Lord Clive.

In 1765, he went back to India for the last time to sort out the corruption and disorder in Bengal, but made many enemies in the process. He was recalled to England to face a parliamentary enquiry, which censured him for his methods. Although the Commons unanimously agreed that he had rendered great service to his country, he was upset by the damage done to his dignity and reputation, and committed suicide in 1774.

HISTORY REPEATS ITSELF

On 10 November 1918, the Armistice ending World War One was signed by representatives of Germany and the Allied forces in a railway carriage at Compiegne in France, 40 miles outside Paris. On 22 June 1940, Adolf Hitler insisted that French representatives sign an armistice with Germany in the same railway carriage, parked at the same spot.

Greatest height achieved by the waters of the Emperor Fountain at Chatsworth, Derbyshire, built in 1844 to celebrate a visit by the Tsar of Russia

PAST PUZZLES

What connects journalist and former MP Martin Bell with
The Times crossword puzzle?
Answer on page 153.

THE HANGMAN'S TABLE OF WEIGHTS

When hanging was still a method of execution, James 'Hangman' Barry, author of *The Business Side of Hanging*, drew up a list to help his colleagues judge the correct drop height for the victim. The lighter the condemned, the longer the drop:

Prisoner's weight	Drop
14 stone (196 lbs)	8 ft 0 in
13 1/2 stone (189 lbs)	8 ft 2 in
13 stone (182 lbs)	8 ft 4 in
12 1/2 stone (175 lbs)	8 ft 6 in
12 stone (168 lbs)	8 ft 8 in
11 1/2 stone (161 lbs)	8 ft 10 in
11 stone (154 lbs)	9 ft 0 in
10 1/2 stone (147 lbs)	9 ft 2 in
10 stone (140 lbs)	9 ft 4 in
9 1/2 stone (133 lbs)	9 ft 6 in
9 stone (126 lbs)	9 ft 8 in
8 1/2 stone (119 lbs)	9 ft 10 in
8 stone (112 lbs)	10 ft 0 in

GLOBAL WARMING

The hottest day on record in the UK was 10 August 2003, when the temperature reached 38°.1C (100.6°F), in Gravesend, Kent.

HISTORIC WORDS

[The king] sent his men all over England into every shire and had them find out how many hundred hides there were... or what land and cattle the king himself had in the country or what dues he ought to have from the shire. And he had a record made of how much land his archbishops had and his bishops and abbots and earls...so very narrowly did he have it investigated that there was no single hide nor indeed was one ox or one cow or one pig left out that was not put down in his record.

**An account by historian Orderic Vitalis of
the writing of the *Domesday Book*, 1086**

QUOTE UNQUOTE

A great prince was dependent upon my pleasure, an opulent city lay at my mercy; its richest bankers bid against each other for my smiles; I walked through vaults which were thrown open to me alone, piled on either hand with gold and jewels. Mr Chairman, at this moment I stand astonished at my own moderation.'
Sir Robert Clive, Governor of India, 1763,
defending himself against claims of corruption

TWENTIETH-CENTURY CRISES

The Abdication Crisis (1936)

On 10 December 1936, King Edward VIII did the unthinkable and gave up his throne to marry the woman he loved, American divorcee Wallis Simpson. In a broadcast to his subjects, he offered his continued service to his country: 'If at any time in the future I can be found of service to His Majesty in a private station I shall not fail.' However, the ex-King and his wife were to be virtually exiled. The new King, George VI, refused to take his brother's calls. A financial settlement was offered to Edward on the condition that he never return to live in the UK. No member of the royal family attended the wedding and the couple – by now the Duke and Duchess of Windsor – were told that their descendants could not inherit the title HRH. When Edward made an ill-judged visit to meet Hitler in 1937, it soured relations even further, and a rumour began that the King might be restored to the throne should Germany ever win a war with Britain. Edward's intentions were probably quite the opposite, but he was in great danger of being used by the Nazis as a pawn. After some bad-tempered negotiation with his family, the Duke finally accepted the governorship of the Bahamas and took up residence there in 1940, out of reach of the Germans. Edward retired from the post in 1945 and moved to France, where he and his wife lived out their days. Despite the long years of frosty relations, Prince Charles and the Queen both visited the Duke before he died in 1972, and his body was flown back to England and buried in Windsor. The Duchess died in 1986 and was buried beside her husband.

THE NEW BOY

Britain's youngest bishop was Prince Frederick, Duke of York and Albany and the second son of George III, who was elected Prince-Bishop of Osnabrück on 27 February 1764, at the age of six months (196 days). He resigned 39 years later.

---

84 *Length, in inches, of the vellum roll on which the Poor Law of 1601 was written*

Surnames first came into use in England in the twelfth century, because of a growth in population after the Norman Conquest and the difficulty of identifying people correctly in the Domesday Book. In Wales, surnames did not appear much until the early seventeenth century, due to the tradition of oral pedigrees being handed down by the Bards.

The origin of a surname falls into one of five categories:

Patronymic This indicates a relationship. For example, Johnson, John or Johns mean 'son of John', and Dickinson means 'son of Richard'. Sometimes forenames simply became surnames without the 'son', such as James or Paul. Scottish names beginning with Mc come into this category: McDougal is 'son of Dougal'. The Irish prefix O' does the same job. Welsh patronymic names stem from the Welsh 'ap' or 'ab' meaning 'son of', from which we get Pugh (ap Hugh, son of Hugh), Price (ap Rhys) and Bunyan (ap Onion) and Bowen (ab Owen).

Locative These names – such as the classic Norman 'de' – show where a man lived or came from, or in some cases that he owned that place. The 'de' was later dropped from many names, leaving just the place name itself. So names such as Kent, Derbyshire, Devonshire and Lancashire indicate a place of origin.

Topographical Describes the place of residence. Many are obvious: Tower, Field, Fieldhouse, Hill, Churchman, Cross, Ridge, Shaw, Marsh, Atwell, Green and Wood. More unusual are Holt (a wood), Combe (tree-covered hill), Kerr or Carr (marshy ground) and Yeo (West Country for brook).

Occupational These are easily recognised: Weaver, Tailor, Baker, Miller, Turner, Clerk, Carpenter, Dyer and, of course, the ubiquitous Smith are all self-explanatory. There were also blacksmiths, whitesmiths, goldsmiths, silversmiths, locksmiths, greensmiths (coppersmiths), knifesmiths (from which comes Naismith) and tinsmiths. Some are not quite so obvious – for example, Fletcher for a maker of arrows, Telford for a maker of iron and Tranter for a carrier. Surnames are also derived from offices held, such as Knight, Squire, Burgess, Yeoman, Freeman, Bishop, Lord and Abbot.

Nicknames Short, Long, Round, Small, Little and Large indicate physical stature, while Black, Grey, White and Reed (red) describe colourings, as do Fairfax and Blundell for blondes. Ballard was a bald man and Giffard had fat cheeks; Cripps was curly-haired and Hoare was hoary or grey. Spelling, of course, has always been as the writer heard the name, so Reed is the same as Read and Rede, and Clerk and Clark are interchangeable, as are Taylor and Tailor, Shepherd and Sheppard and so on.

*Richard the Lionheart's press officer tries out some ideas
for a Crusades recruitment poster.*

THE END OF THE PEER SHOW

Lawrence Shirley, the fourth Earl Ferrers, was the last British peer to be executed, and was hanged rather than beheaded, the latter being the usual punishment for a nobleman. Renowned for his foul temper and violent behaviour, Ferrers shot dead his steward after a misunderstanding, and was arrested the next day. He was tried in the House of Lords, where he vigorously defended himself by claiming to be insane (some said there was insanity in the family). However, when the Lords dismissed this as a poor excuse, he heartily agreed and said his friends had put him up to it. He was duly sentenced to death by hanging. The public were agog, and the route to the gallows was so crowded with spectators that it took Ferrers three hours to get there from the Tower, not least because he brought a huge retinue with him, including a cavalry escort. He gave the traditional tip to the executioner's assistant by mistake, and had to wait while the executioner tussled with the assistant to retrieve his fee. When the Earl finally met his end, the fall failed to kill him, and the hapless assistant was forced to pull on his feet to complete the task.

THE ORIGINS OF ALBION

Of the many names that Britain has enjoyed, 'Albion' is perhaps the most romantic. *The Oxford Companion to the English Language* explains that the word probably has a shared Celtic and Latin root, meaning 'white' or 'the white land', possibly referring to the cliffs of Dover that would greet new arrivals. Others suggest that it means 'the world' or simply 'the land'. It has also been suggested that Albion comes from the name of a giant (a son of the sea god, Neptune), from England's first Christian martyr (Alban), or from Princess Albia, the oldest of the 50 daughters of the King of Syria who settled in Britain. Albion was misappropriated in 1793 by Marquis de Ximenes, who first used the words 'perfidious Albion' in a poem, a phrase that was seized upon and re-used in the Napoleonic recruiting drive of 1813.

QUOTE UNQUOTE

The one duty we owe to history is to rewrite it.
Oscar Wilde, playwright

FIRST BRITISH NOBEL PRIZE WINNERS

1902	Sir Ronald Ross	Medicine	Discovery of how malaria enters an organism
1903	Sir William Cremer	Peace	Founder of Workmen's Peace Association
1904	Lord Rayleigh	Physics	Discovery of argon
	Sir William Ramsay	Chemistry	Discovery of inert gases
1906	Sir JJ Thomson	Physics	Research into electrical conductivity of gases
1907	Rudyard Kipling	Literature	For remarkable narration
1908	Lord Rutherford	Chemistry	Disintegration of elements, chemistry of radioactivity
1915	Sir William and Sir Lawrence Bragg	Physics	Analysis of crystals by means of X-rays
1917	Charles Barkla	Physics	Discovery of characteristic X-radiation of elements
1921	Frederick Soddy	Chemistry	Chemistry of radioactive substances and occurrence and nature of isotopes
1922	Francis Aston	Chemistry	Work with mass spectograph
1922	Archibald Hill	Medicine	Discovery relating to heat production in muscles

THE SEVEN KINGDOMS OF BRITAIN

When Britain was settled by the Angles, Saxons and Jutes after the
Romans left, it comprised the following kingdoms:

East Anglia • Essex • Kent • Mercia
Northumbria • Sussex • Wessex

MADE IN BRITAIN

When	Who	Invented what
1901	Hubert Cecil Booth	Electric vacuum cleaner
1913	Harry Brearley	Stainless steel
1916	Ernest Swinton	The tank, the first effective tracked and armoured fighting vehicle
1924	John Logie Baird	Television
1930	Frank Whittle	Patented the idea of a jet engine for aircraft
1932	George Carwardine	Anglepoise lamp
1941	John Whinfield and James Dickson	Terylene
1955	Christopher Cockerell	Hovercraft

FAMILY HISTORY

The last surviving person in Britain whose parents were born in the
eighteenth century was Alice Grigg of Kent, who died in April 1970.
Her father, William, was born on 26 October 1799.

HISTORIC WORDS

Lady Beavale told me some anecdotes of the Royal children, which
may one day have an interest when time has tested and developed
their characters. The Princess Royal is very clever, strong in body and
in mind; the Prince of Wales weaker and more timid, and the Queen
[Victoria] says he is a stupid boy; but the hereditary and unfailing
antipathy of our Sovereigns to their Heirs Apparent seems this early
to be taking root, and the Queen does not much like the child. He
seems to have an incipient propensity to that sort of romancing which
distinguished his uncle, George IV. The child told Lady Beavale that,
during their cruise he was very nearly thrown overboard, and was
proceeding to tell her how when the Queen overheard him, sent him
off with a flea in his ear, and told her it was totally untrue.

From the diary of Charles Greville, politician, 22 January 1848

Skara Brae, *Isle of Orkney*
Discovered in 1850, contains eight houses that were probably home to 40 or 50 people. Inhabited around 3100-2500BC.

Maes Howe, *Isle of Orkney*
Built before 2700BC. Forty metres long by seven metres wide, entrance aligned to the southwest to be illuminated by the midwinter equinox. A large mound covers a stone-built passage and a large burial chamber.

The Stones of Stennes, *Isle of Orkney*
Dating back to 2900BC. Consists of two sites: the Ring of Brogar (Temple of the Sun) and Ring of Stennis (Temple of the Moon).

Great Orme, *Llandudno, Wales*
Six kilometres of tunnels one metre high by two metres wide, the largest prehistoric mining complex in the world, featuring a 4000-year-old opencast mine.

Maiden Castle, *Dorset*
Massive hill fort dating back to 3500BC, overrun by the Roman Second Legion August in 44AD. Covers 47 acres, with high, steep ramparts. Excavation uncovered 38 bodies, each of which had been laid to rest with a flagon of beer and a joint of meat.

Flag Fen, *Peterborough, Cambridgeshire*
Dating back to 3000BC, featuring prehistoric timbers and reconstructed roundhouses. The site was waterlogged, and leaves, twigs, flowers and pollen were also retrieved. The site also houses the Seahenge timbers, found in Norfolk.

Avebury Stone Circle, *Wiltshire*
Circular earthwork c. 2600–3000BC, 400 metres wide surrounded by a ditch, inside which is a circle of standing stones, surrounding two more stone circles. In total comprises around 600 megaliths.

West Kennet Long Barrow, *Wiltshire*
Same period as Stonehenge. Comprises a 100-metre mound containing five chambers opening off a central passage. The entrance is marked by massive stones arranged along a north-south line.

Dover Boat, Dover Museum, *Dover*
One of the most important maritime discoveries in our history. About 3550 years old and strong enough to cross the Channel, carrying supplies and passengers, it was propelled by paddles.

As chosen by Dr Francis Pryor, archaeologist, Bronze Age expert and one of the team that discovered Flag Fen.

MODERATION IN ALL THINGS

When Lionel, Duke of Clarence, married his Italian fiancée in 1368, her dowry included the truffle hills of Alba. The white truffles that they yielded were considered to be an aphrodisiac, and a quantity of them was provided at the wedding feast. Sadly the Duke partook of so many that he died of a surfeit before he was able to find out if they worked.

POPULATION OF WALES

43AD	250,000 (Roman invasion of Britain)
1190	160,000
1290	300,000
1400	200,000 (after the Plague)
1536	278,000
1620	360,000-400,000
1770	500,000
1851	1,163,000
1914	2,523,500
1925	2,736,800
1939	2,487,000
1971	2,731,000
2001	2,938,000

STRANGE CUSTOMS

Allendale Tar Barrels

This tradition has managed to evade all manner of health and safety regulations and is still being celebrated well into the twenty-first century. On 31 December, the Northumberland town of Allendale holds a Burning the Old Year Out ceremony. A collection of 'guisers', local men in fancy dress, set out on a modest pub crawl and festive procession around the town. Around 11.30pm, after imbibing sufficient courage, the men and their followers gather in the market square – by now filled with villagers – each carrying a cut-down tar barrel on his head. Each barrel is 15 inches deep, filled with tar, wood and paraffin-soaked shavings. The barrels are lit and the Tar-Barrellers proceed, led by a band and with the crowd in tow, until at the stroke of midnight, the cry goes up: 'Be damned to he who throws last!' and the blazing barrels are thrown on to a pile of fir branches to set it alight. The custom is thought to have started around 1860, when the same ceremony was enacted with candles; but a blustery wind kept blowing the candles out, so a bold soul suggested a more robust inflammatory device.

GREAT BRITONS

Gordon of Khartoum (1833-1885)

Charles Gordon is best known for meeting a sticky end in Khartoum. But before that tragic event he had a long and illustrious military career. He became a gentleman-cadet at the age of 15 and was commissioned into the Royal Engineers in 1852. His first active service was in the Crimea at the Siege of Sebastopol, after which he was decorated by the French for bravery. In 1860 he volunteered for service in China, where his unit of Engineers was assigned the task of strengthening the defences of Shanghai against the Taiping rebels. In 1864, the Chinese asked the British for a replacement for Frederick Townsend Ward, who had been killed while clearing the rebels out of Shanghai, and Gordon was given the job. He took command of Ward's 'Ever-Victorious Army' and successfully quashed the rebellion, after which he became known as 'Chinese' Gordon. He gained a reputation for being courageous and modest, and when he was lavishly rewarded by the Emperor, he shared the money among his men.

In 1874, by now a full Colonel, he was sent to command the troops in the Sudan. He left there in 1880 to become Private Secretary to the Viceroy of India, and from 1882-1884 was Commander of the British Forces in Mauritius. But in 1884, after the revolt of Mohammed Ahmed, 'the Mahdi', against the Anglo-Egyptian government, Gordon was sent back to Sudan to save the British troops, by withdrawing them down the Nile to Egypt. But he considered it too dangerous, and was afraid that to abandon Khartoum would leave the Sudanese in the hands of the Mahdi's men, who would enslave them. So he disobeyed orders and soon found himself under siege in Khartoum. When the news reached England, the public demanded that their hero be rescued. At first the government refused, intending that he should return home. But Gordon felt honour-bound to help the Sudanese and settled in for a long and bloody fight, expecting that help would arrive. Eventually, under pressure from the public and the Queen, an expedition was sent to rescue him. But it was too late. After a siege of 320 days, Gordon was betrayed by his Egyptian lieutenant and shot dead by the Mahdi's followers on 26 January 1885. Two days later, the English relief army reached Khartoum.

Half a league, half a league,
Half a league onward,
All in the valley of Death
Rode the six hundred.
'Forward, the Light Brigade!'
Charge for the guns!' he said;
Into the valley of Death
Rode the six hundred.

'Forward, the Light Brigade!'
Was there a man dismay'd?
Not tho' the soldier knew
Some one had blunder'd:
Their's not to make reply,
Their's not to reason why,
Their's but to do and die:
Into the valley of Death
Rode the six hundred.

Cannon to right of them,
Cannon to left of them,
Cannon in front of them
Volley'd and thunder'd;
Storm'd at with shot and shell,
Boldly they rode and well,
Into the jaws of Death,
Into the mouth of Hell
Rode the six hundred.

Flash'd all their sabres bare,
Flash'd as they turn'd in air,
Sabring the gunners there,
Charging an army, while
All the world wonder'd:
Plunged in the battery-smoke
Right thro' the line they broke;
Cossack and Russian
Reel'd from the sabre-stroke
Shatter'd and sunder'd.
Then they rode back, but not,
Not the six hundred.

Cannon to right of them,
Cannon to left of them,
Cannon behind them
Volley'd and thunder'd;
Storm'd at with shot and shell,
While horse and hero fell,
They that had fought so well
Came thro' the jaws of Death
Back from the mouth of Hell,
All that was left of them,
Left of six hundred.

When can their glory fade?
O the wild charge they made!
All the world wonder'd.
Honour the charge they made!
Honour the Light Brigade,
Noble six hundred!

The Charge of the Light Brigade, **Lord Alfred Tennyson**

The Charge of the Light Brigade was made at Balaclava on 25 October 1854. A vaguely worded order delivered by an excitable young officer ordered the Light Brigade of Cavalry, without any support, to try to prevent the Russians carrying off some British naval guns that had been abandoned by the Turks.

A blunder, which has never been properly explained, caused the Light Brigade instead to charge down the westernmost valley where there was a whole division of Russian cavalry, and six battalions of infantry supported by 36 guns. Of the 636 that advanced, 157 died and many others later died of their wounds. It has been described as the worst conducted military action in British history.

TOO MANY COOKS

Between 30 October 1683 and 6 February 1685, there were eight British heads of state and future heads of state alive, the most to be alive simultaneously. They were Charles II, James II, William and Mary, Anne, George I and George II, as well as Richard Cromwell, the second Lord Protector.

WRONG MAN FOR THE JOB

George II will perhaps go down in history as one of England's most bad-tempered kings. Inheriting the throne from his father, George I, who had been reluctant to leave his native Germany to take the English throne, George II set about out-grumping the father he detested. Once on the throne, George brought dullness to his court, insisting on perfect etiquette and punctuality at all times. He would hold long, boring mono-logues on his own military exploits, his favourite subject after the state of the economy.

George, like his own father, hated his eldest son, Frederick. 'Our first-born is the greatest ass, the greatest liar, the greatest canaille and the greatest beast in the whole world and we hearti-ly wish he was out of it,' har-rumphed the King (although some claim these to be the Queen's words). Described by his son as having an insatiable sexual appetite, George II took a German mistress, whom he commanded his wife to like. When Queen Caroline began to die a lingering death, the King merely asked her how she expected him to sleep when she would not lie still (although he

admitted to being upset when she did die). He was so rude to his courtiers that those he spurned formed their own club called the Rumpsteak Club. But George just got grumpier. 'I am sick to death of all this foolish stuff and wish with all my heart that the devil may take all your bishops, and the devil take your Minister, and the devil take your parliament and the devil take the whole island provided I can get out of it and go to Hanover,' he declared.

George's reputation was saved by war: at the age of 60, he fought alongside his troops, leading his army to victory against the French at Dettingen in 1743. This boosted his popu-larity, and he took advantage of this to make a visit to his beloved Hanover, a trip that became so lengthy that the Duke of Newcastle had to per-suade him to come home. George's final triumph was to outlive his wretched son, and refuse to pay the debts that Frederick left behind. But his reputation was to suffer one final indignity: a long-term suf-ferer of constipation, George II died of a heart attack while sit-ting on the lavatory.

YOUNGEST KINGS AND QUEENS OF BRITAIN

Who	Age at accession	Year of accession	Length of reign
Edward the Martyr	12 or 13	975	3 years
Athelred	9	978	38 years
Edgar the Peaceful	15	959	16 years
Henry III	9	1216	56 years
Edward III	14	1327	50 years
Richard II	10	1377	21 years
Henry VI	8 months 25 days	1422	39 years
Edward IV	18	1461	22 years
Edward V	12 (never crowned)	1483	2 months
Henry VIII	17	1509	38 years
Edward VI	9	1547	6 years
Lady Jane Grey	15 (never crowned)	1553	9 days
Victoria	18	1837	63 years

WHO WAS THE REAL SHERIFF OF NOTTINGHAM?

History has long enjoyed representing the Sheriff of Nottingham as an out-and-out villain. In fact, Nottingham didn't actually have a sheriff until 1449, although there had been a Sheriff of Nottingham*shire* since the Conquest. However, that doesn't mean the story is mere fiction. In the supposed time of Robin Hood, while King Richard was away on the Crusades (1190-94), Nottingham was in a state of flux. Justiciar Longchamp (who technically was working for both Prince John and King Richard) tried to keep control of the region, but succeeded only some of the time. From 1190-91, however, Nottingham fell under the control of Prince John, who brought in his own man, a medieval enforcer called William de Briwere.

De Briwere was one of the most hated and feared men in England and (a rare thing) a favourite of both Richard and John. Richard had appointed him as one of Longchamp's 'supervisors' while he was on Crusade, but Longchamp began to exceed his authority soon after Richard left, and de Briwere quickly shifted his loyalties to John.

De Briwere was everything the stories make the Sheriff out to be – greedy, vain and insanely ambitious. Even the corrupt church hated him, largely because he liked to kidnap the clergy's mistresses and ransom them back again to raise money. In 1210, the people of Dorset and Somerset, where de Briwere was also Sheriff, offered King John a large amount of money to get rid of him. John took the money and simply moved de Briwere to another county to continue his work, which can only have strengthened his terrible reputation.

Year in the 1800s when Sunderland FC became the first British football team to undertake an overseas tour

THE FLYING MONK

In the annals of flight, many are accorded the accolade of 'first man to fly' – the Wright Brothers, of course, and Sir George Cayley, who built the first glider, not to mention the Montgolfier Brothers and their hot-air balloon of 1783.

But there is another claimant for this title, a young Englishman called Eilmer, who allegedly first flew 700 years before the Montgolfiers – in 1010. Eilmer was a monk in the ancient Wiltshire town of Malmesbury. According to the famous local historian William of Malmesbury, who was writing just after Eilmer's lifetime, the monk fastened wings to his hands and feet, launched himself off a tower, probably that of the old Abbey, and flew 200 feet before coming to earth with a bump, breaking both his legs. But this was no impromptu escapade – Eilmer had been studying the jackdaws that lived around the abbey, and had worked out how they used the air currents to glide. On recovering from his first failure, he began planning a second attempt, this time adding a tail to his wings for stability. Sadly the abbot decided enough was enough, and Eilmer's flying days were over.

It is quite possible that what Eilmer had invented was the hang-glider. A stained glass window commemorating Eilmer's achievement can be seen to this day in Malmesbury Abbey.

QUOTE UNQUOTE

If we had not invented, during the winter of 1938/39, a new alloy and a new furnace to make it which hardened the propeller casing of the Spitfire, and made it 50mph faster than the Messerschmitt instead of 50mph slower, it is surely likely that Hitler would have won the war.
Conrad Russell, historian and Liberal Democrat peer

I PROMISE TO PAY THE BEARER

The oldest surviving printed Bank of England note was made out to... a value of £555, and is dated 1793.

The largest notes printed by the Bank of England... are worth £100 million, but are for accounting purposes only, not for public issue.

The highest denomination note issued for public use... was worth £1,000, and was first printed in 1725. It was last issued in 1943 and ceased to be legal tender on 16 April 1945.

The lowest denomination note issued for public use... was for 10 shillings, issued in 1914. It ceased to be legal tender in June 1920.

OLD PICTURE, NEW CAPTION

*Lord Malmesbury demonstrates the time-saving benefits
of his new double-ended sideburn trimmer.*

PAST PUZZLES

How many drams is an ounce?
Answer on page 153.

GREAT BRITISH FIRSTS

1495	The first dry dock in the world opens in Portsmouth.
1604	The first English dictionary is published, entitled *A Table Alphabeticall* by Robert Cawdrey.
1704	The first alphabetical encyclopedia in the world is published, *Lexicon technicum*, edited by John Harris.
1738	A local midwife in Charlemont, Ireland performs the first Caesarian on record in the UK; mother and child survive.
1744	The first golf club in the world opens, The Honourable Company of Edinburgh Golfers.
1769	Honoretta Pratt is the first person to be cremated in the UK.
1777	The first boat in the world to have an iron hull is built in Yorkshire.
1779	The world's first iron bridge, designed by Abraham Darby III, is completed in Shropshire.
1794	A house in Redruth, Cornwall is the first to be lit by gas, which is piped in from an enclosed coal fire.

The illegitimate offspring of Britain's monarchs:

• **Henry I** produced so many illegitimate children that it is hard to keep count, but there were at least nine sons and 11 daughters, although some historians count as many as 25. The sons included Robert Fitzroy, Earl of Gloucester.

• **Henry II** had 12 illegitimate children, including William, Earl of Salisbury, and Geoffrey, who became Archbishop of York.

• **Richard I** is known to have at least one bastard son, Philip.

• **John I** had 12 illegitimate children, including a daughter, Joan, who married Llywelyn the Great, ruler of Wales.

• **Edward I** had one illegitimate son, John de Bottetourt, who served in his father's expeditions to Gascony and Scotland.

• **John of Gaunt**, the son of Edward III, had several children by Katharine Swynford: John, Henry, Thomas and Joan Beaufort. John of Gaunt later married Katherine and in 1397, their cousin, Richard II, legitimised all four of them 'as if you were born of a lawful union'. However, the phrase 'except royal dignity' was later added to the document, to prevent their having a claim to the throne. John became the Marquess of Dorset and Somerset, Henry was Bishop of Winchester and Thomas was Earl of Dorset and Duke of Exeter. John Beaufort's great grandson Henry VII ignored the interpolated phrase and seized the throne in 1485, using this line of succession as his justification.

• **King Edward IV** had a bastard son called Arthur Plantagenet, who was imprisoned in the Tower for some kind of plot. Unfortunately he was so overcome on being pardoned by the King that he died of excitement.

• **Henry VIII** had several illegitimate children, including his favourite, Henry Fitzroy. The boy was made a duke as well as Lord High Admiral, Lord Warden of the Marches and Lord Lieutenant of Ireland.

• **Charles II** produced 16 bastards with several mistresses, including Charles Fitzroy, Duke of Southampton and Cleveland, Henry Fitzroy, Duke of Grafton, and George Fitzroy, Duke of Northumberland. He also had two sons by Nell Gwynn, Charles and James Beauclerk; Charles was created Duke of St Albans. The King's first illegitimate son James, Duke of Monmouth, had aspirations to the throne, which Charles did not support. On Charles's death, Monmouth tried to seize the crown anyway, but was imprisoned and hanged.

• **William IV** had a longstanding love affair before he became King, with a Mrs Dorothy Jordan, who bore him 10 children. When William became King, he made the eldest son, George Fitz-Clarence, the Earl of Munster, Viscount FitzClarence and Baron Tewkesbury, and gave titles to the other children.

GOOD IDEAS

The first five patents awarded in Britain

Engraving and printing the King's head on documents
Nicholas Hillyard *5 May 1617*

Locks, mills and other river and canal improvements
John Gason *1 July 1617*

Oil for suits of armour
John Miller and John Jasper Wolfen *3 Nov 1617*

Tunnels and pumps
Robert Crumpe *9 January 1618*

Making maps of English cities
Aaron Rathburne and Roger Burges *11 March 1618*

These were the patents awarded when the system was first formalised, although it could be argued that the very first patent was awarded in 1449 by Henry VI to John of Utyman for making the coloured glass for the windows of Eton College

---

HISTORIC WORDS

After this time the part of Britain inhabited by the Britons lay wholly exposed to the ravages of invaders. All their armed men, their military supplies, and the whole flower of their vigorous young warriors had been removed by the reckless adventures of despots, never to return; and the people had no knowledge of the skills of warfare. As a result they suffered a sudden invasion from two warlike peoples across the sea, the Irish from the north-west and the Picts from the north, and their plight continued for many years...

Plagued by these peoples, the Britons sent messengers to Rome with letters bearing their tearful entreaties for help and their promise of permanent subjection to Rome if the enemy should be repelled. An armed legion was quickly assigned to them, sailed to the island, engaged with the enemy, and inflicted great losses on them, driving the survivors out of their allies' territory. Having freed the Britons from this cruel oppression, they urged them to build a defensive wall across the island from sea to sea to keep out the enemy; and the legion returned home in great triumph.

But when their former enemies saw that the Roman forces had left, they soon arrived again in their ships and invaded their borders, cutting down and trampling on everything that met their advance, like reapers mowing ripe corn.

The Britons are invaded by the Irish and Picts, and ask Rome for military help. From the *Ecclesiastical History of the English People, Book I, Chapter 12*, written by the Venerable Bede, c.730

**The Hervey family can lay
claim to some of the country's
most creative rogues and eccentrics:**

John, Lord Hervey of Ickworth had manners so effeminate that he was referred to by Alexander Pope as Lord Fanny. Lord Hervey had a wife, mistresses and male lovers, and once turned his wife and children out of the family home so that he could give it to his lover, Stephen Fox.

Augustus Hervey, son of the second Earl of Bristol, was married at the age of 16, but kept it secret for 20 years so that his wife would not lose her job as maid of honour to the Princess of Wales. Hervey joined the navy and used his position to seduce a vast number of women, including some of the inhabitants of a convent in Odivellas. Addicted to amorous risks, he once had to lie still under his lover's bedclothes while her husband bid her goodnight. He acknowledged only one child, born to his mistress Kitty Hunter, although the boy was killed while serving in the Navy.

Frederick Hervey, the fourth Earl of Bristol and the Earl-Bishop of Derry once dropped a tureen full of pasta from a tower in Siena on to a Corpus Christi procession. He was also once imprisoned in a tower in Milan. When he died in Italy, the crew of the ship that was to transport his corpse refused to carry it, so the body was disguised in a packing case and sent home as an antique statue.

Victor Hervey, the sixth Marquess of Bristol, once drove his car into a taxi rank to satisfy his curiosity as to whether a taxi would buckle like a concertina. He discovered that they did. As well as writing gossip columns, in which he referred to himself as 'Mayfair Playboy No. 1', he worked (unsuccessfully) as a gun-runner in the Spanish Civil War, sold arms to China and lived as a tax exile in Monaco.

As Voltaire was to say: 'When God created the human race, he made men, women – and Herveys.'

QUOTE UNQUOTE

*Whosoever, in writing a modern history, shall
follow truth too near the heels, it may
haply strike out his teeth.*
Sir Walter Raleigh, explorer

The editorial committee agreed that they should publish Shakespeare's first play, but his suggested title of 'Whoops, There Go My Pantaloons' would need some work.

THE FIRST CHEMICAL WEAPON

The great secret weapon of the Middle Ages was known as Greek Fire, a stream of flaming oil that, like modern napalm, burned furiously on contact and could not be put out. First used by the Byzantines in the seventh century, the recipe was a very closely guarded secret, so closely that, after a while, even the Byzantines forgot how to make it. The secret, however, was probably not in the mixture itself, but in its delivery. According to medieval sources, the highly potent mixture was pressurised in a large metal container, and then shot out at the enemy like a flamethrower. But although the Byzantine recipe was lost, a form of Greek Fire was successfully used by the Arabs until the early medieval period.

Its first recorded use on British soil was at King Richard's siege of Nottingham Castle in 1194, his first act on returning from Crusade. History assumes that he brought the deadly weapon with him from his encounters with the Muslim armies, particularly at the siege of Acre, at which it was rained down with great effect on the Christian armies. However, the besiegers of Nottingham had been using it since the beginning of the attack, and Richard and his men didn't get there until two days later. So we cannot be sure whose idea it really was – unless bad news travels fast.

BRITAIN'S IMPERIAL TERRITORIES

1497 ....Newfoundland	1815.............................Mauritius
from 1607 ....USA	1815 ....Ionian Islands
1609..............................Bermuda	1819 ....British Antarctica
1624 ....St Christopher	1819.............................Singapore
1625 ....Barbados	1821 ....Gold Coast
1627 ....St Vincent	1825 ....Tasmania
1629................................Bahamas	1826................................Burma
1632..........Antigua and Barbuda	1829 ....Western Australia
1632 ....Montserrat	1833 ....Falkland Islands
1638 ....Belize	1835.....................South Australia
1638 ....Turks Caicos Islands	1835.....................South Australia
1650................................Anguilla	1838 ....Pitcairn
1651 ....Surinam	1839.....................................Aden
1655...............................Jamaica	1840......................New Zealand
1661..................................Gambia	1851 ....Victoria
1661............St Helena, Ascension	1859......................Queensland
and Tristan da Cunha	1861..................................Nigeria
1670......................Rupert's Land	1868..................................Lesotho
1670....................Cayman Islands	1870 ....Tanzania
1672 ....Virgin Islands	1874 ....Fiji
1704...............................Gibraltar	1878 ....Cyprus
1708...............................Minorca	1882.....................................Egypt
1713......................Nova Scotia	1884 ....Bechuanaland
1713....................New Brunswick	1884 ....British Somaliland
1757 ....India	1884.............British New Guinea
1763......................Prince Edward	1887 ....Kenya
Island	1887...............................Maldives
1763................................Ontario	1887 ....Vanuatu
1763 ....Quebec	1888 ....Brunei
1763.............................Dominica	1888 ....Uganda
1763.............................Grenada	1888 ....Rhodesia
1763.................................Florida	1889..................................Malawi
from 1786......................Malaysia	1890 ....Swaziland
1787 ....Sierra Leone	1892 ....Kiribati
1788.................New South Wales	1892...................................Tuvalu
1793.................British Columbia	1893 ....Solomon Islands
1793.................Vancouver Island	1898.....................................Sudan
1795 ....South Africa	1900......................................Tonga
1796................................Guyana	1917...............................Palestine
1800.....................................Malta	1917 ....Transjordan
1802...........Trinidad and Tobago	1918 ....Iraq
1807.........................Heligoland	1919................................Namibia
1814............................Seychelles	1919....................Western Samoa
1814 ....St Lucia	1919 ....Nauru
1815 ....Ceylon	1947................................Pakistan

Number of the airship that set off from Cardington in 1930 and later crashed, 101
in the world's first air disaster

THE OTHER PATRON SAINT OF ENGLAND

Edmund, the last king of the East Angles, is one of Britain's forgotten heroes. Around the time of his reign in the ninth century, England was suffering periodic raids by the Vikings, although they usually returned to their homeland to enjoy their spoils. But by 865 they were settling rather than leaving, and were becoming more rapacious and violent. Edmund decided it was time to make a stand. The Danes often negotiated with the local kings, but Edmund refused to concede to their unreasonable demands. In 869 a battle was fought at Hellesdon at which Edmund was captured and executed. Reports vary as to how he was killed; some say that he was shot to death with a great quantity of arrows, others that he was flayed, tortured and beheaded, after which soldiers found a wolf standing guard over his severed head. When his body was reburied in 915, it was found to have suffered very little decay, and Edmund began to attract a cult of hero-worship. Within a few decades, he was regarded as one of England's patron saints, until his memory was displaced by St George. But Edmund's name lives on in the town where he was reburied, formerly known as Bedricsworth. In the fine tradition of calling a spade a spade, it was renamed Bury St Edmunds.

PAST PUZZLES

Why would huffcap, mad dog, angel's food and dragon's milk be bad for you?
Answer on page 153.

WHO ARE YOU CALLING A DUNCE?

John Duns Scotus (c.1266 – 1308) was a Scottish Franciscan who lectured in Oxford and Paris and was considered a highly sophisticated thinker for his time. He is considered to be the first person to drive a wedge between philosophy and theology, paving the way for the growth of scepticism in the fourteenth century. It seems strange, therefore, that he gave rise to the word 'dunce'. Scotists – a name given to those following his line of thinking – were also referred to as 'Dunsmen' or 'dunses', which, despite today's connotations, at first referred to someone who made 'impossibly ingenious distinctions', and could be taken as a compliment. However, it became a term of contempt after Duns's death, as his followers became best known for being deeply conservative and for blindly resisting change or new ideas.

In 1557, the Vatican City published the first edition of its *Index Librorum Prohibitorum*, a list of censored books. It was updated regularly and writers of all nationalities were censored for immoral or blasphemous works, including the following British writers:

Thomas Hobbes	1649-1703	All his works
Francis Bacon	1668	*The Arrangement and General Survey of Knowledge*
John Milton	1694	*The State Papers*
Joseph Addison	1729	*Remarks on Several Parts of Italy*
Richard Steele	Not known	*An Account of the State of the Roman Catholic Religion*
John Locke	1734-1737	*An Essay Concerning Human Understanding*
Daniel Defoe	1743	*History of the Devil*
Samuel Richardson	1744	*Pamela*
David Hume	1761-1827	All his works
Edward Gibbon	1783	*Decline and Fall of the Roman Empire*
Laurence Sterne	1819	*A Sentimental Journey through France and Italy*
Oliver Goldsmith	1823	*An Abridged History of England.*
John Stuart Mill	1856	*Principles of Political Economy*
Andrew Lang	1896	*Myths, Ritual and Religion*

STRANGE CUSTOMS

Weighing the Mayor

Every year in High Wycombe, a mayor is elected. But before he or she can take office, they have to be weighed – in public. The tradition is unique to High Wycombe and was thought to date back to a pointed remark made by Queen Elizabeth I about the size of the town's dignitaries. However, records of the actual ceremony date back only to Victorian times. The unfortunate mayor sits on a flimsy chair suspended from an equally flimsy looking tripod, underneath a dial that reveals his or her weight. In the spirit of fairness, the charter trustees, honorary burgesses and outgoing mayor are also weighed. To add insult to injury, the Macebearer shouts out the weight for all to hear, adding 'and some more' if they have gained weight since last year. Jeers and whistles duly accompany any extra poundage, to protest that the undignified dignitary has grown fat at the townspeople's expense. A weight loss, on the other hand, is greeted with applause, as the mayor has clearly been working him or herself to the bone.

The most interesting aspect of the story of King Arthur is perhaps the evolution of the story itself; how a local warlord, who was almost certainly not a true Briton, came to be such a central part of our country's history.

Countless historians and writers have constructed different theories, and the trouble lies in disentangling fact from fiction. As Philip Howard says in his book *The Royal Palaces*: 'The basic trouble about both Camelot and King Arthur is that they have been so covered with intricate layers of romance, and superstition, and religious mysticism, and historical propaganda, and archaeological wishful thinking, and sheer dottiness that it is hard to know whether underneath the mountain of literature there really ever was a hard kernel of fact.' Adrian Gilbert, author of *The Holy Kingdom*, claims that Arthur was, in fact, two British kings: Arthur I of Warwickshire, a fourth-century king; and his sixth-century descendant, Arthur, King of Glamorgan. Over the centuries, the two lives have merged to create the legendary King Arthur.

A character named Artorius is first mentioned in writing by Nennius, a ninth-century Welsh monk, in his *History of Britain*. Even then, the accounts were suspicious: Artorius allegedly fought in 12 great battles, had 12 knights and single-handedly slew 960 men in the Battle of Badon around the year 500. Geoffrey of Monmouth continued the story in his *History of the Kings of Britain*, which was completed around 1136. But critics claim that he was creating an epic history for his country, rather than sticking to the facts. As historian Edward Gibbon explained: '[Arthur's] romance, transcribed in the Latin of Jeffrey of Monmouth...was enriched with the various, though incoherent, ornaments which were familiar to the experience, the learning, or the fancy of the twelfth century.'

In 1190 the monks at Glastonbury exhumed the 'remains' of Arthur and Guinevere, finding an oak coffin and a cross, inscribed 'Here lies buried the renowned King Arthur in the Isle of Avalon'. The coffin contained the remains of a tall man and a golden-haired woman. However, it is assumed this was a hoax.

The tale was continued in the twelfth century by Chretien de Troyes, and later by Sir Thomas Malory, an English knight, who based his *Le Morte d'Arthur* on a French book. By this time Arthur's world was one of courtly life and chivalrous acts, a far cry from his real origins.

Some of the real kings of England have been known to adopt Arthur as their hero. Edward III built a circular banqueting hall to hold a round table, and formed the Order of the Garter to include the most valiant knights of his time, in an undisguised tribute to the legendary king. Henry VIII painted his own face on Arthur's image. Even parts of the present-day Houses of Parliament are decorated with scenes from Arthur's life. None of this embellishment has prevented Arthur worshippers over the centuries from wanting to find the remains of his court, and various sites have been suggested (and excavated), from Tintagel Castle in Cornwall to Carlisle and London. None has been proven. But the lack of hard evidence has only fuelled the legend. Arthur now stands as an indelible example of how we want our heroes to be: strong, morally upright leaders, who demonstrate courage in adversity, unwavering love for their queen and a willingness to defend England to the death.

QUOTE UNQUOTE

Hark the herald angels sing
Mrs Simpson's pinched our king.
Children's rhyme during the 1936 abdication crisis

GREAT BRITISH FIRSTS: TRAINS AND BUSES

1803	Richard Trevithick builds the first steam locomotive to pull wagons, which ran on the Penydarren Railway in Wales. It was originally built to drive a steam hammer.
1825	The first passenger steam railway opens, running from Stockton to Darlington.
1829	The first scheduled bus service, horse-drawn, runs from Marylebone Road to Bank. The fare was one shilling for the whole journey, 6d for any intermediate stage.
1829	George and Robert Stephenson build The Rocket steam engine, the ancestor of the modern locomotive.
1830	William Huskisson MP becomes the first train accident fatality: he is run down by the Rocket at the opening of the Liverpool and Manchester Railway on 15 September, as he crosses the track without looking both ways.
1831	The first self-propelled omnibus runs from Stratford in London to the City.
1847	The first double-decker bus, built by Adams & Co of Bow, London, takes to the city's streets. Those riding on top were less comfortable, but paid half-fare.
1890	The first electric underground railway in the world opens in London, the City and South London Railway.
1903	The first municipal motor omnibus service in the world is inaugurated on 12 April between Eastbourne railway station and Meads in East Sussex.
1909	The world's first bus conductress is Kate Barton, who worked for her father's bus company in Nottinghamshire.

Name of school	Founded
King's School, Canterbury, Kent	597
King's School, Rochester, Kent	604
St Peter's, York	627
St Alban's	948
King's School, Ely	970
Norwich School	1096
High School of Glasgow	1124
Westminster	1179
High School of Dundee	1239
Royal Grammar School, Worcester	1291

HISTORIC WORDS

At half past four drove in open landau and four with Arthur, Leopold, and Jane C., the Equerries riding. We drove round Hyde and Regent's Parks, returning by Constitution Hill, and when at the Garden Entrance a dreadful thing happened... The Equerries had dismounted, [John] Brown had got down to let down the steps and Jane C. was just getting out, when suddenly someone appeared at my side, whom I at first imagined was a footman, going to lift off the wrapper. Then I perceived that it was someone unknown, peering above the carriage door, with an uplifted hand and a strange voice, at the same time the boys calling out and moving forward. Involuntarily, in a terrible fright, I threw myself over Jane C., calling out, 'Save me,' and heard a scuffle and voices! I soon recovered myself sufficiently to stand up and turn round, when I saw Brown holding a young man tightly, who was struggling. They laid the man on the ground and Brown kept hold of him till several of the police came in. All turned and asked if I was hurt, and I said, 'Not at all.' Then Lord Charles, General Hardinge, and Arthur came up, saying they thought the man had dropped something. We looked, but could find nothing, when Cannon, the postillion, called out, 'There it is,' and looking down I then did see shining on the ground a small pistol! This filled us with horror. All were as white as sheets, Jane C. almost crying, and Leopold looked as if he were going to faint.

It is to good Brown and to his wonderful presence of mind that I greatly owe my safety, for he alone saw the boy rush round and followed him! When I was standing in the hall, General Hardinge came in, bringing an extraordinary document which this boy had intended making me sign! It was in connection with the Fenian prisoners!

From the diary of Queen Victoria, 29 February 1872

Age of Percy Goring when he died in 2001, the last-known British veteran to serve at Gallipoli

PILOTS WIN PRIZES

At the early twentieth century, aviation was very much in its infancy, but Lord Northcliffe, owner of the *Daily Mail*, believed it was crucial to Britain's commercial prosperity. He offered a series of cash prizes for pilots to complete a number of flying milestones:

1908	£100 Quarter-mile out/return	*H Farman*
1909	£1,000 Cross-Channel flight	*M Bleriot*
1909	£1,000 Circular mile	*JTC Moore-Brabazon*
1910	£10,000 London–Manchester	*M Paulban*
1910	£100 Second cross-channel	*M de Lesseps*
1910	£1,000 Best cross-country aggregate	*M Paulhan*
1910	£50 cup Paris–London	*JB Moissant*
1911	£10,000 Round Britain	*A Beaumont*
1912	£105 cup Aerial Derby	*T Sopwith*
1913	£105 cup Aerial Derby	*G Hamel*
1914	£105 cup Aerial Derby	*WL Brock*
1919	£210 cup Aerial Derby	*Captain GW Gathergood*
1919	£10,000 Transatlantic flight	*Sir J Alcock and Sir A Whitten Brown*

PAST PUZZLES

What were dredge, maslin, berevechicorn and bollymong used for?
Answer on page 153.

STRANGE CUSTOMS

Whuppity Stourie

In Lanark in Strathclyde every 1 March, a group of children run 'sunwise' around the parish kirk, whirling paper balls on string around their heads and beating each other with them as they run in a ceremony known as Whuppity Stourie. They are accompanied by the church bells, which are silent from October to February, but begin ringing again on 1 March. The first boy and girl to complete three circuits win a cash prize, and the rest have to scramble for coins scattered on the ground by the provost. Until the 1900s, the race was more boisterous; young men sped around the church, whirling their caps, then set off for a fight with the lads of Lanark. But the town magistrates banned this version of the ceremony and replaced it with something more innocent. The tradition is thought to have originated in the whipping of penitents around the church, or was perhaps a ritual to exorcise evil spirits, who travel in clouds of dust (stour). In Scottish folklore, Whuppity Stourie is the name of a bad fairy, who is defeated only if her victim can guess her name.

QUOTE UNQUOTE

*Today 23 years ago dear Grandmama died. I wonder
what she would have thought of a Labour Government.*
King George V, after inviting
Ramsay MacDonald to form Britain's first
Labour government in 1924

WHO WAS THE ADMIRABLE CRICHTON?

James Crichton was a Scotsman who once issued a challenge to the intellectuals of Paris that he would answer any question put to him on the subjects of art and science. He also offered to deliver his answers in any of twelve languages, from Syriac to Slavonian. Reports of him frequenting taverns and spending his time gaming, hawking or larking about did not bode well. But on the appointed day, Crichton sparred with the learned minds of Paris, acquitting himself so well that the president of the college praised Crichton for 'the many rare and excellent endowments which God and nature had bestowed upon him' and presented him with a diamond ring and a purse of gold. The prodigy celebrated by engaging in a tilting match at the Louvre, surrounded by admiring young ladies.

Crichton was born around 1560 and studied at St Andrews University. By the age of 20, he could speak 10 languages and was accomplished in science as well as in various social skills such as dancing, riding and the playing of musical instruments. On a tour of Europe, aged 20, he challenged the intellectuals of Rome to test his learning, and submitted himself for questioning to the Pope, several cardinals, doctors of divinity and a number of professors of science, who were overwhelmed by his abilities. He repeated the exercise in Padua, with equal success. He went on to prove his physical prowess by publicly dispatching a murderous gladiator in Mantua, earning the gratitude of the Duke of Mantua. The Duke then asked Crichton to reform his wayward son, Vincentio, which Crichton attempted by satirising the young man in a play, in which he acted all 15 parts himself. But Vincentio was not amused, and set upon Crichton at a carnival on 1 July 1582. Crichton handed him his sword and invited him to do what he must. Vincentio ran him through. Crichton's short but colourful life was immortalised by several writers, including Sir Thomas Urquhart, in an account of his life (1651) and a novel by William Ainsworth (1867). JM Barrie wrote a play, *The Admirable Crichton*, in 1902, but it tells the quite different tale of a British butler shipwrecked on a desert island.

OLD PICTURE, NEW CAPTION

Lord Melchett hoped no one would notice that the building costs of his new west wing had been filed under 'Sundries'.

THEY DIED YOUNG

**The youngest kings and queens of Britain
to be cut down in their prime:**

Monarch	Age at death	Date	Cause
Margaret of Scotland	7 yrs 5 mths 18 days	1290	Frail health
Edward V	12 yrs 10 mths	1483	Murdered
Edward VI	15 yrs 8 mths 25 days	1553	Tuberculosis
Edward the Martyr	16 yrs	978	Murdered
Lady Jane Grey	16 yrs 4 mths	1553	Executed

HISTORIC WORDS

'…bruised beans, two modii, chickens, twenty, a hundred or two hundred eggs, if they are for sale there at a fair price…8 sextarii of fish-sauce…a modius of olives.'

A letter to the slave of Verecundus, a prefect at the Roman settlement of Vindolanda, one of the main military posts in the north of Britain before the building of Hadrian's Wall.
The shopping list dates back to around 100AD and is one of the oldest surviving handwritten documents to be found in Britain. It was written on a wafer-thin slice of wood, using carbon ink and a quill-type pen.

MADE IN BRITAIN

When	Who	Invented what
1839	James Nasmyth	Steam hammer
1843	John Calcott Horsley	First Christmas card (for Sir Henry Cole)
1845	Robert Thomson	Patented the rubber tyre
1855	Robert Yeates	Tin-opener
1864	George Harrington	Dental drill
1870	James Starley	Penny farthing bicycle
1876	Samuel Plimsoll	The Plimsoll line
1876	Alexander Graham Bell	Patented the telephone
1892	James Dewar	Vacuum flask (also invented cordite and liquid hydrogen)
1892	R Crompton and H Dowsing	First electric room heater

WHAT'S THAT IN OLD MONEY?

1 guinea = 21 shillings
1 pound = 20 shillings
1 crown = 5 shillings
1 shilling = 12 pence
1 penny = 4 farthings

THE ANGLO-SAXON CHRONICLE

This early chronicle of Britain is an essential reference for any historian, as it traces the history of the country from the birth of Christ to 1154. It was thought to have been commissioned by the scholarly Alfred the Great, as a way of repairing the damage done to English life by the Vikings, and instilling some sense of his country's history into his subjects. There are seven surviving manuscripts, the last entry for which, in 1154, is the also the last known document to be written in Old English. It brought together the work of Anglo-Saxon monks and priests, including the Venerable Bede, who began writing down their history when Christianity returned to the country in the sixth century. These writings were collected together in the ninth century, and new writings added, up to the mid-twelfth century, as the monasteries carried on the work after Alfred's death. The many different entries range from one-liners to poems and long and lyrical passages, including such stirring stories as the arrival of Hengist and Horsa, and Alfred's last wars against the Danes. It remains a document of enormous historic, linguistic and literary importance.

110 *Depth, in metres, of the Old Mine at Marston, Northwich, in which the Tsar of Russia dined in 1844*

THE VICTORIA CROSS

The Victoria Cross (VC) was created by Queen Victoria in 1856, but was backdated to 1854 to allow it to be awarded to participants in the Crimean War. It is bestowed for actions in the presence of the enemy, although six have been awarded for actions 'under circumstances of extreme danger', such as launching a rescue in adverse conditions. Here are a few facts:

- The crosses are made from the metal of guns captured from the Russians in the Crimean War. They are made by Hancocks and Co of Burlington Gardens, in London.
- The VC has been awarded 1,355 times in its history.
- VCs were at first not awarded posthumously, but that rule was changed in 1920.
- The chances of surviving a heroic act worthy of a Victoria Cross are estimated at one in 10.
- Charles Lucas was the first recipient of the Victoria Cross.
- The largest number of VCs won in a single day was 24, at the second relief of Lucknow on 16 November 1857.
- The largest number won in a single action was 11, at Rorke's Drift on 22 January 1879.
- The ribbon holding the medal was originally crimson for the Army and blue for the Navy, but was changed to crimson for all the services in 1918.
- Three men have won the VC twice: they are Arthur Martin-Leake, Noel Chavasse and Charles Upham.
- Andrew Fitzgibbon and Thomas Flinn were the youngest recipients, aged 15. Fitzgibbon was a drummer boy, but engaged the enemy in hand-to-hand combat at Cawnpore during the

Indian Mutiny of 1857. Flinn was a hospital apprentice at the capture of the Taku Forts in China in August 1860. He attended to the wounded under heavy fire and was himself wounded.
- Three pairs of fathers and sons have been awarded the VC, and eight brothers.
- Three Canadians awarded the VC all lived on the same street in Winnipeg, which was renamed Valour Road in their honour.
- It was possible for a VC to be forfeited if the soldier were considered to have brought dishonour on himself, which usually meant he was a deserter or a thief. However, some former heroes were stripped of their honour for relatively minor offences. King George V insisted that once a VC had been awarded, it should never be removed. In 1920 he wrote: 'Even were a VC to be sentenced to be hanged for murder, he should be allowed to wear his VC on the scaffold.' No VC has been taken away from its owner since 1908.
- Since 1945, the VC has been awarded only 12 times.
- The last VC was awarded in 2005 to Private Johnson Beharry, aged 25, for his bravery in the war against Iraq.

TREASURES OF THE DEEP

In March 2005, a team of amateur archaeologists uncovered the find of a lifetime – the remains of a shipwreck believed to date back to 1,300BC. Discovered in a mere 60 feet of water off the coast of Devon, the find offered an unprecedented insight into the behaviour of Britain's Bronze Age inhabitants. The South West Maritime Archaeological Group who found the remains, retrieved a cauldron hanger, bronze swords and axes and a solid gold torc, which suggest that the vessel was a warship rather than a trading ship. Sadly there was no trace of the wooden ship itself, which had long since disintegrated, but the artefacts were in exceptionally good condition. Only two other vessels of a similar age have been found, and it is possible that the Devon ship is one of the oldest shipwrecks to be found off the British coast.

NO PLACE LIKE HOME

The 10 most common placenames in Britain:

Name	No of occurrences
Newton	150
Blackhill	136
Castlehill	128
Mountpleasant	126
Woodside	112
Newtown	110
Burnside	107
Greenhill	105
Woodend	101
Beacon Hill	95

THREE THINGS WALTER RALEIGH DIDN'T DO

...lay down his cloak for Queen Elizabeth. The myth probably originated with imaginative historian Thomas Fuller, and was embroidered by Sir Walter Scott.

...introduce the potato to England. According to John Gerard's 1597 book 'Herball', the potato was first grown in Italy in 1585, and was introduced to England from there by Sir Francis Drake in 1586.

...introduce tobacco from America. Walter Raleigh never actually landed on mainland America, and Europe's first tobacco was brought from Brazil to France by Andre Thevet in 1556. The first tobacco to reach England came in on the ship of Sir John Hawkins c.1564. Sir Walter Raleigh was first introduced to tobacco by Sir Francis Drake some 20 years later.

112 *Amount of ale, in gallons, brewed and consumed each week in the household of Dame Alice de Bryene, Suffolk, in 1412*

NOT LONG TO REIGN OVER US

Ten monarchs who spent the shortest time on the throne

Lady Jane Grey	9 days
Aelfweard	16 days
Swein Forkbeard	40 days (recognised as king but not crowned)
Edward V	2 months 17 days
Edmund Ironside	7 months (proclaimed king in London only)
Harold II	9 months
Edward VIII	11 months (not crowned, abdicated)
Richard III	2 years 2 months
Edward the Martyr	2 years 9 months
Harold I	3 years

QUOTE UNQUOTE

The best history is but like the art of Rembrandt; it casts a vivid light on certain selected causes, on those which were best and greatest; it leaves all the rest in shadow and unseen.
Walter Bagehot, nineteenth-century economist

WITCHES, PROPHETS AND MYSTIC MEN

Count Louis Hamon

William John Warner was born in Ireland in 1866, and fled his life of poverty in Ireland to become one of the world's most successful seers. Adopting the name Count Louis Hamon, he headed first for India, where he learned palmistry and refined his hobbies of astrology and numerology. Anticipating his own good fortune, he moved to London, adopted the name of Cheiro, and proceeded to amaze all of fashionable society with his palm readings and predictions. These included the disgrace of Oscar Wilde, the election of Arthur Balfour as prime minister and the exact date of Queen Victoria's death. He gained particular fame by predicting an assassination attempt on the Shah of Persia in 1900, and was rewarded with the Order of the Lion and the Star. On meeting the future Edward VIII as a child, Cheiro predicted that he would abdicate due to an unsuitable marriage. He also warned a man named WT Stead not to travel by water in April 1912 (Stead duly cancelled his ticket for the maiden voyage of the *Titanic*), and advised Lord Carnarvon not to enter the tomb of Tutankhamun. Unfortunately Carnarvon ignored the warning, and died shortly afterwards. Cheiro was also a newspaper editor, writer, radio presenter and war correspondent. It is said that he was a lover of Mata Hari and a spy. He spent his last years in Hollywood, where he wrote screenplays and gave psychic readings over the radio. He died in 1936.

TEENAGE PARENTS

Monarchs who had children exceptionally young

In 1382 **Henry IV** and **Mary de Bohun** had a son, Edward, when Henry was 15 and Mary was 13. The child died after four days.

In 1457 **Margaret Beaufort** gave birth to a son, the future Henry VII, at the age of 13 years, 7 months and 28 days.

In 1678, Mary, the future **Queen Mary II**, gave birth to a stillborn child at the age of 16. She had two more stillborn children with her husband, William, in the next two years, but the couple never produced a surviving heir.

In 1239 **Eleanor of Provence**, wife of Henry III, gave birth to a son, the future Edward I, at the age of 16.

In 1330, **Edward III** became a father at the age of 17, when his 19-year-old wife, Philippa, gave birth to a son, Edward, the Black Prince.

In 921, **Edgiva**, wife of Edward the Elder, gave birth to a son, the future Edmund I, aged 16.

GREAT BRITISH FIRSTS

1886	The world's first oil tanker, the *Gluckauf*, is built in Tyneside.
1901	The first radio signals (comprising the morse code for 'S') are sent across the Atlantic, from Cornwall to Newfoundland, by Guglielmo Marconi.
1901	The first cinema in the UK opens, Mohawk's Hall, London.
1902	Harry Jackson becomes the first man in the UK to be convicted on fingerprint evidence.
1905	The first UK beauty contest is held in Newcastle-upon-Tyne.
1908	Old-age pensions are introduced in the UK by Chancellor of the Exchequer, Lloyd George.
1908	The first officially recognised powered flight to be made in the UK is completed by American Samuel Franklin Cody, who flew 1,390 feet and was airborne for 27 seconds.
1912	The first advert in the UK for a brassiere is published in *The Queen*, 'a necessity for those of generous build'.
1915	Edith Smith is the first policewoman in the UK to be given full powers of arrest.
1916	Daylight saving begins in UK: clocks go forward one hour.
1919	The first purpose-designed aircraft carrier, HMS Hermes, is launched (although not commissioned until 1923).

---

114 *Amount, in thousands of pounds, found aboard a Spanish treasure ship when it was seized by Sir Francis Drake in 1587*

On 14 November 1698, ship-owner Henry Winstanley completed the construction of a lighthouse on the treacherous Eddystone rocks, on which he had earlier lost two ships. He took it upon himself to build the lighthouse to prevent further losses, and completed it in spite of being captured by a French privateer halfway through the project. When critics claimed the lighthouse would never survive the winter, Winstanley rashly boasted that his greatest wish was to be safely tucked up in his lighthouse during the worst storm in history.

On 26 November 1703, the east coast of Britain was lashed by weather more severe than had ever before been recorded. It began around midnight, and brought winds so strong that men and animals were lifted from the ground and carried through the air. The roofs were torn from over 100 churches, 15,000 sheep were drowned in floods near Bristol, and 800 houses were destroyed. Ships anchored off the coast were blown against the rocks and each other, and 8,000 sailors were drowned in one night. Four hundred windmills were also destroyed; some blew over, but others caught fire from the sheer friction of their spinning sails.

Fires broke out in many villages, but the terrified inhabitants were too afraid to leave their homes and brave the storm. They were eventually forced to flee, as the fierce winds fanned the flames and created an inferno. Church steeples and chimney stacks came down everywhere, often killing those who lay or walked underneath.

Much of the devastation occurred in the east of the country, although London suffered too. Every one of the 120 church steeples in the capital was damaged, and trees were ripped from the ground in the city's parks.

As well as the loss of sailors, the storm devastated the British navy, which lost hundreds of vessels, including four men-of-war. Witnesses reported seeing one ship at Whitstable in Kent being lifted right out of the sea and dropped on dry land. Parliament was particularly concerned at the damage done to its navy, and large numbers of workmen were recruited as quickly as possible to rebuild the country's fleet. Prisoners, including prisoners of war, were offered the chance to redeem their crimes by replacing the many sailors lost in the storm.

As for Henry Winstanley, his wish was granted, although not quite in the way he had envisaged. The day before the storm, he took a party of men out to Eddystone Rocks to make some repairs. By the time the gales had abated, there was nothing left of his wooden lighthouse, or its inhabitants, save for a few pieces of bent iron protruding from the rock.

OLD PICTURE, NEW CAPTION

*Alexander Graham Bell learns that he is being held in a
queue and will be answered shortly.*

HISTORIC WORDS

Infatuate Britons, will you still proclaim
His memory, your direst, foulest shame?
Nor patriots revere?

Ah! when I hear each traitorous lying bell,
'Tis gallant Sidney's, Russell's, Vane's sad knell,
That pains my wounded ear.

John Keats, English Romantic poet
*Lines written on 29 May,
the anniversary of the
restoration of Charles II.*

What do you call a collection of Boy Scouts?
Answer on page 153.

A SHORT HISTORY OF CENSORSHIP

William Caxton, the father of the British printing industry, set a good example by censoring his own publications, replacing 'arse' with 'buttocks' for example, in his translation of Malory's *Le Morte d'Arthur* in 1485. But others were less willing to follow his example and the authorities soon felt compelled to step in.

Henry VIII issued a list of banned books in 1529, including Thomas More's *Utopia*. He also prevented the importing of books written in English, in particular the translations of the *Bible* by William Tyndale and Miles Coverdale.

In 1557, the Catholic Church began its *Index Librorum Prohibitorum*, in which it listed works that it had censored. The list was frequently republished and at its height listed 5,000 banned books, including works by Samuel Richardson and Daniel Defoe.

Elizabethan authorities forbade 'obscenities' on stage, and decreed that plays could not include 'matters of religion or of the governance of the estate of the common weale'. Among others, satirist and playwright Ben Jonson and his cast were sent to jail for performing *The Isle of Dogs* (1597) and *Eastward Ho!* (1605).

Throughout the seventeenth century, the producers of unlicensed publications risked having their ears cropped, noses slit and cheeks branded with the letters S and L ('seditious libeller').

The Civil War saw such severe restrictions placed upon the press that the poet Milton felt compelled to write *Areopagitica* in 1644, protesting against censorship and calling for greater freedom of the press.

The direct political attacks by novelist Henry Fielding – then the manager of the New Theatre in London – on the royal family and the government in 1737 led to the Licensing Act of the same year, which gave the Lord Chamberlain unprecedented power to suppress theatrical works. Theatrical censorship by the Lord Chamberlain was not abolished until 1968.

Editor Thomas Bowdler produced an edition of Shakespeare's plays in 1818 with all the supposedly rude bits cut out, which gave rise to the term 'to bowdlerise'.

In 1960, the Crown prosecuted Penguin Books for publishing the unexpurgated version of *Lady Chatterley's Lover*. The publisher's acquittal was seen by many as a blow to the establishment.

COALS TO NEWCASTLE

A few of Britain's bolder exports:

- The Premier Drum Company of Leicester sold four shipments of tom-toms to Nigeria, and shifted a consignment of maracas to South America.
- Permaflex of Stoke-on-Trent sold £50,000 petroleum to the Arabs in the form of lighter fluid.
- Associated Health Foods of Surrey sold 100 tonnes of wholewheat pasta to Italy.
- Eastern Sands and Refractories of Cambridge shipped 1,800 tonnes of sand to Abu Dhabi.
- Unilever Export sold 100 cases of Batchelor's Vesta Chow Mein to Hong Kong.
- Bunce Ltd of Wiltshire sold a snow-plough to Dubai.

American merchant Timothy Dexter did once send coals to Newcastle, which happened to arrive just as the city ground to a halt amidst a coal strike. He made a huge profit.

BRITISH RECORD-BREAKERS

While working as a waitress at Alexandra Palace in London, 16-year-old Dolly Shepherd stepped from the audience at *Buffalo Bill's Wild West Show* to take the place of his wife, who had been injured during a display of blindfold shooting. In return, Samuel Cody (Bill's real name) introduced her to parachuting.

Dolly – whose real name was Elizabeth – made her first jump at the age of 17, after just 30 minutes of instruction and thereafter took it up as a career, taking part in demonstrations as part of a team. On 9 June 1908, Dolly entered the record books by carrying out the world's first mid-air rescue by parachute. The parachute of her fellow jumper, Louie May, became tangled as the girl clung to the trapeze bar suspended below the balloon. Dolly got the girl out of her harness and ordered her to wrap herself around her rescuer as they fell 11,000 feet, using Dolly's single parachute. They both survived the landing, although Dolly was temporarily paralysed by the fall, but was cured by controversial electric shock therapy. Dolly worked as a parachutist for another four years before giving it up and joining the Women's Air Auxiliary Corps as a driver mechanic. She died in 1983 at the age of 96, having seen the first man walk on the moon, an astonishing contrast to her own airborne career. She also flew with the Red Devils a few years before she died. Dolly's daughter, Molly Sedgwick, celebrated her 83rd birthday in 2003 by making a parachute jump with the Red Devils from 13,000 feet. She raised £6,224 for charity.

KINGS IN WAITING

Eldest sons who should have been king but never quite made it

Edward, *son of Edward III*
Died 1376, a year before
his father.

Edward, *son of Henry VI*
Died 1471, as did his father.

Edward, *son of Richard III*
Died 1484, a year before
his father.

Arthur, *son of Henry VII*
Died 1502; his brother Henry
suceeded in 1509.

Henry, *son of James I*
Died 1612, 13 years before
his father; his brother suceeded
instead, becoming Charles II.

James, *son of James II*
James II was replaced as king by
his daughter and son-in-law
Mary and William, thus moving
the line of succession sideways.

Frederick, *son of George II*
Died 1751, nine years before
his father; his son became king.

QUOTE UNQUOTE

History will be kind to me, for I intend to write it.
Winston Churchill, prime minister and author

KITCHEN EQUIPMENT

There should be a provision of good cauldrons to boil large cuts of meat, and a great number of moderate-sized ones for making pottages and for other cooking operations, and great suspended pans for cooking fish and other things and a great number of large and ordinary sized boilers for pottages and other things and a dozen good big mortars...And you will need some twenty large frying pans, a dozen great kettles, fifty pots, sixty two-handled pots, a hundred hampers, a dozen grills, six large graters, a hundred wooden spoons, twenty-five holed spoons, both large and small, six pot-hooks, twenty oven shovels, twenty roasters, both those with turntable spits and those with spits mounted on andirons. You should not put your trust in wooden skewers or spits, because you could spoil all your meat, or even lose it; rather you should have six score iron spits which are strong and thirteen feet long; and you need three dozen other spits which are just as long but not as thick, in order to roast poultry, piglets and water birds...And besides this, four dozen slender skewers for doing glazing and for fastening things.

**Instructions for
feeding the royal
household in 1403**

Thomas Paine (1737-1809)

Thomas Paine was the son of a staymaker who became one of the country's most famous radical writers. Dismissed from his job for demanding a pay increase for himself and his colleagues, he left for America, where he published a number of outspoken pamphlets. One of the best known of his early publications was *Common Sense* (1776), which advocated the separation of America from Britain and sold around 100,000 copies in its first few months. Paine also opposed slavery and was in favour of the emancipation of women. In 1787 he returned to England, where he published his most famous work, *The Rights of Man*. In it he praised the new constitutions of America and France and criticised that of England, and laid out his ideas on tax reform, family allowances, maternity grants and other liberal and far-sighted measures. He despised the flowery writing style of his contemporaries, particularly Edmund Burke, and wrote instead in a plain and simple style unusual for the time. 'Mr Burke should recollect that he is writing history, not plays', he sneered. His later pamphlet, *The Age of Reason* (1793), attacked Christianity, which damaged his reputation in England, and effigies of him were burnt in the street. He was tried in absentia for treason, which meant that he could never return. He eventually sailed back to America, where he lived out his last years. When he died in 1809, his bones were retrieved by fellow pamphleteer William Cobbett, who intended to restore Paine's remains to England, but managed to mislay the bones before completing his task.

HISTORIC WORDS

But today came the news that she [the Titanic] had gone down with over a thousand souls on board within three hours of the collision, and very shortly after wireless messages broke off. Perhaps it is Nature's most effective tour de force since Sodom and Gomorrah; for she was the last word in ostentatious luxury, and the very embodiment of our insolent claims to have conquered the elements. Our civilisation has been very properly put in its place, as Roman civilisation was at Pompeii.

From the diary of
Sir Alan Lascelles, 16 April 1912

Lunched at the Thirty. There was much talk of the Titanic tragedy. Lady Dorothy Nevill said that the wreck was a judgement from God on those idle rich people who want all earthly luxuries even on the water. She observed: 'I am told they even had a garden!'

From the diary of
Marie Belloc Lowndes, 18 April 1912

OUT OF SIGHT, OUT OF MIND

In 1788, the newly acquired land of Australia became a penal colony for England's criminals. Convicts were taken from the courthouse or the overflowing jails and sent to Australia to serve out their sentence. By 1830 over 50,000 convicts had been sent overseas.

The sentence of deportation was intended for serious crimes such as murder, but it was often misused. The first deportees included a nine-year-old petty thief and an 82-year-old woman accused of perjury. It also didn't take the government long to realise that this was an easy way for them to get rid of people they considered troublesome – such as

the **Tolpuddle Martyrs**. The Martyrs were six agricultural labourers from Dorset, who, impoverished by their low wages, set up a union in Tolpuddle to give their fellow labourers better bargaining power. The authorities were keen to suppress any trade union activity, and the six were falsely accused of taking secret oaths, tried and sentenced to seven years' deportation.

But the authorities had gone too far. The sentence sparked off angry demonstrations across the country and Parliament was forced to issue a pardon, although it was three years before the men returned home. Transportation was brought to an end in 1868.

QUOTE UNQUOTE

Let us cling to our legends, sir... they are the spiritual side of facts.
Harley Granville Barker, actor, producer and writer

FEUDAL RANKS

King: Owns all the land, gives away parcels of land (fiefs), in return for future service.

Lords: Hold the land given by the king, which they lease to lesser ranks, who in turn supply the lords with money or knights should the need arise.

Vassals: Pay homage to the lords and lease land to the knights.

Knights: Lease land from vassals, and offer their services in return, when required.

Squires: Young knights-in-training, usually aged 14-21.

Seigneurs: Lords of the manor, a manor being the smallest plot of land.

Villeins/serfs: Live on and are bound to a manor or fief. They pay rent to the lord that owns it.

Servants: The lowest in rank. Workers owned by the wealthy, including nobility and wealthy merchants.

GREAT BRITISH FIRSTS

1919	The first flight out of the UK, London to Paris, costs £21.
1919	The first international airmail from the UK travels from London to Paris.
1921	Marie Stopes opens Britain's first birth-control clinic.
1927	The first transatlantic telephone links open between London and New York.
1932	The first book tokens in the UK are issued.
1945	Family allowance is issued for the first time at a rate of five shillings per child.
1946	The first woman to wear a bikini in the UK is Maisie Dunn, on her honeymoon, on the beach at Newquay.
1946	The first television licence is issued, costing £2.
1954	The first four-minute mile is run by Roger Bannister in Oxford in three minutes 59.4 seconds.
1957	Elizabeth II makes the first sovereign's Christmas speech.
1961	The oral contraceptive is introduced to the UK.
1962	The Brighton Metropole becomes the UK's first legal casino.
1978	The world's first test-tube baby is born in England.

THE FINAL DROP

The number of hangings in England, Scotland and Wales, in the last 10 years of the death penalty:

1955	9
1956	0
1957	3
1958	5
1959	4
1960	7
1961	4
1962	2
1963	2
1964	2

ALL CHANGE

On 9 February 1909, a German military band played 'God Save the King' 16 times in succession on the platform of Rathenau Railway Station in Brandenburg. The lengthy performance was to cover the embarrassment of King Edward VII, who was struggling to get into his Field-Marshal's uniform before emerging.

---

122 *Age of Thomas Parr, England's oldest man, when he married for the second time in 1605*

In modern times, almost every European country has devoted greater energy and resources to the study of its own national history than to the study of Europe as a whole... The problem is particularly acute in Great Britain, where the old routines have never been overturned by political collapse or national defeat. Until recently, British history has generally been taken to be a separate subject from European history – requiring a separate sort of expertise, separate courses, separate teachers, and separate textbooks. Traditional insularity is a fitting partner to the other widespread convention that equates British History with English History... The English are not only insular; most of them have never been taught the basic history of their own islands. Similar attitudes prevail in universities. Honourable exceptions no doubt exist; but Britain's largest history faculty did not start teaching 'British history' until 1974; and even then the content remained almost entirely English. The students rarely learn anything about Ireland, Scotland or Wales. When they take examinations in 'European history', they are faced with a few optional questions about Eastern Europe and none about Britain. The net result can only be a view of the world where everything beyond England is alien.

Norman Davies, *Europe: A History*

THE VENERABLE BEDE

The Venerable Bede (c.673-735) was born near Wearmouth in the north of England and at the age of seven went to live in the nearby monastery. The library there was one of the best in Britain, and Bede began the studies that would make him one of Britain's most important historians.

A few years later Bede transferred to a monastery in Jarrow, where he began work on the earliest complete history of Britain: *Historia Ecclesiastica Gentis Anglorum*, the *Ecclesiastical History of the English People*. Unlike some early chroniclers, Bede did not like to imagine or embellish his stories, which makes his records more useful than many, more fanciful, histories. His chronicles begin with the arrival of Caesar in 55BC and conclude with the state of the nation in 731.

His work was unusual for treating the country as a single entity; at the time, England was still divided into kingdoms such as Mercia and Wessex, but Bede looked forward to a time when the country would be united, and would be 'English' from top to bottom. Alfred the Great, who ruled from 871-99, shared Bede's vision of a united England, and had his work translated from Latin to English. However, it would be two centuries before Bede's vision would begin to be realised, when Alfred's grandson became the first king to rule the whole of England.

WELL-KNOWN MIDDLE NAMES

Jeremy John Durham [Paddy] Ashdown: *Leader of Liberal Democrat Party, 1988-99*

Nancy Witcher Astor: *First woman MP to take her seat in House of Commons*

Wystan Hugh Auden: *Poet*

'Jack' John Whitaker Straw: *Labour Foreign Secretary 2001-04*

Alan John Percivale Taylor: *Historian*

Michael Mackintosh Foot: *Leader of Labour Party 1980-83*

John Denton Pinkstone French: *Commander of British Expeditionary Force 1914-15*

Hugh Todd Naylor Gaitskell: *Leader of Labour Party 1955-63*

James Augustine Aloysius Joyce: *Novelist*

Pelham Greville Wodehouse *Novelist*

Marie Charlotte Carmichael Stopes: *Advocate of birth control*

Evelyn Arthur St John Waugh: *Novelist*

A SCOTTISH KING?

The discovery of some ancient remains under an English motorway in 2005 have led historians to believe that one of the early leaders of the British, might have been a Scot rather than an Englishman. An Iron Age chariot burial was found under the A1M motorway, during the upgrading of the junction with the trans-Pennine M62. Chariot burials were unique to the middle Iron Age (500-100BC) and the find has been dated to around 400BC. The grave was decorated with jewellery and finely worked harness and chariot accessories, and contained the remains of a slender man in his 30s or 40s, about 5ft 9in tall and with very good teeth. The telling fact was the high level of strontium found in the man's bones, which showed that he was not from Yorkshire, where he was buried, but from Scotland. The precious goods found with his skeleton show that he was a king or revered military leader – which in those days were generally the same thing – and first century cattle remains found at the same spot suggest that a tremendous feast was held on the burial ground about 500 years after his death, when the Romans were still in occupation. The feast reinforces the theory that this was the grave of a British king, as archaeologists assume that the hero's grave was used as a rallying point for Britain's tribes to join forces against the Romans.

PAST PUZZLES

What do King Canute and Jane Austen have in common?
Answer on page 153.

HEIRS AND SPARES

The ability to produce plenty of successors has been of vital importance to monarchs through the ages; here are a few who more than met their target:

Monarch	Number of (legitimate) children
Edward the Elder	18
Ethelred the Unready	16
William the Conqueror	10
Henry III	9
Edward I	19
Edward III	13
Edward IV	10
Henry VIII	10 (four stillborn)
James I	9
Charles I	9
James II	20
Anne	18

(only five of these were born alive; two died shortly after birth, two died before they were two, and the last lived to the age of 11)

George II	9 (1 stillborn)
George III	15
Victoria	9

Meanwhile, north of the border...

Robert the Bruce	14

BRITISH RECORD-BREAKERS

The longest-lived British citizen was Eva Morris who died aged 114 – six days short of her 115th birthday – in Stone in Staffordshire, November 2000. Born in Newcastle-under-Lyme in 1885, she shared her birth year with writer DH Lawrence, whom she outlived by 70 years. When Eva was born, Gladstone was in power, and Grover Cleveland was the US president. Widowed in the 1930s, she lived in her own home until she was 107, then moved to a nursing home. She had one child, a daughter, Winnie, who died in 1975 at the age of 102. Eva attributed her long life to whisky and boiled onions.

Tradition has it that Evan James, a weaver from Pontypridd, wrote the words of the Welsh National Anthem one Sunday morning, in January 1856. He set them to a tune composed by his son James James, which it is thought was based on an old harp melody. The date of the song's adoption as the National Anthem is uncertain, but it was probably after the National Eisteddfod at Bangor in 1874. It has been given official status as the National Anthem of Wales:

Hen Wlad fy Nhadau

Mae hen wlad fy nhadau yn anwyl i mi,
Gwlad beirdd a chantorion, enwogion o fri;
Ei gwrol rhyfelwyr, gwlad garwyr tra mad,
Tros ryddid collasant eu gwaed.

Cytgan (Chorus):
Gwlad, gwlad, pleidiol wyf i'm gwlad,
Tra mor yn fur
I'r bur hoff bau,
O bydded i'r heniaith barhau.
Hen Gymru fynyddig, paradwys y bardd,
Pob dyffryn, pob clogwyn, i'm golwg sydd hardd;
Trwy deimlad gwladgarol, mor swynol yw si
Ei nentydd, afonydd, i fi.

Os treisiodd y gelyn fy ngwlad dan ei droed,
Mae heniaith y Cymry mor fyw ag erioed,
Ni luddiwyd yr awen gan erchyll law brad,
Na thelyn berseiniol fy ngwlad.

[Cytgan]

There are various translations but the most literal one of the first verse and chorus is:

Land of my Fathers
The land of my Fathers is dear to me,
A land of poets and minstrels, famed men.
Her brave warriors, patriots much blessed,
It was for freedom that they lost their blood.

Homeland! I am devoted to my country;
So long as the sea is a wall
to this fair beautiful land,
May the ancient language remain.

It is often sung by the English as:

> The land of my fathers is dear unto me,
> The land of the poets, the land of the free,
> Her patriots and heroes, her warriors so brave,
> For freedom their life's blood they gave.
>
> Wales! Wales!
> Pledged am I to Wales
> Whilst seas surround
> This land so proud
> Oh, long may our old tongue remain.

NOT QUITE WINNIE THE POOH

Before the days of *Noddy and Big Ears* and *Thomas the Tank Engine*, books written for children were intended quite simply to put the fear of God into their young readers. Uncompromising moral tales and lectures were written to teach children the difference between good and evil, and the terrible consequences of the latter. The books' titles left little to the imagination: *A Token for Children, being an Exact Account of the Conversion, Holy and Exemplary Lives, and Joyful Deaths of Several Young Children* by James Janeway (1671) was a typical example. Another was *A Token for the Children of New-England, Or, Some Examples of Children in whom the Fear of God was remarkably Budding, before they dyed, in several parts of New England. Preserved and published for the Encouragement of Piety in other Children*, by Cotton Mather (1700).

Books were sometimes aimed at parents, too, such as *A Family Well Ordered, or An Essay to render Parents and Children Happy in one another*. In this particular volume, the author leaves the young reader in no doubt as to the consequences of their bad behaviour:

'The Heavy Curse of God will fall upon those Children that make Light of their Parents...The Curse of God! The Terriblest Thing that ever was heard of; the First-born of Terribles!...Children, if you break the Fifth Commandment, there is not much likelihood that you will keep the rest...Undutiful Children soon become horrid Creatures, for Unchastity, for Dishonesty, for Lying, and all manner of Abominations...And because these undutiful Children are Wicked overmuch, therefore they Dy before their Time. Children, if by Undutifulness to your Parents you incur the Curse of God, it won't be long before you go down into Obscure Darkness, even into Utter Darkness; God has reserved for you the Blackness of Darkness for ever.'

MADE IN BRITAIN

When	Who	Invented what
1806	Ralph Wedgwood	Carbon paper
1814	James Pillans	Blackboard. He also made his own sticks of coloured chalk by grinding up chalk, adding dye, and binding the powder with porridge.
1815	Humphrey Davy	Miner's safety lamp
1815	Samuel Clegg	Gas meter
1821	Michael Faraday	Electric motor
1824	Michael Faraday	Rubber balloons (for use in his experiments with hydrogen)
1828	John and Charles Deane	Diving suit
1830	Joseph Henry	Electric bell: effectively the electric telegraph
1831	Michael Faraday	Electric generator
1831	Michael Faraday	Electric transformer

QUOTE UNQUOTE

It is not possible to create peace in the Middle East by jeopardizing the peace of the world.
Aneurin Bevan, MP, in a speech made at a rally protesting against Britain's role in the Suez dispute

GREAT BRITISH THINKERS

Thomas Hobbes (1588-1679)

Hobbes was allegedly born prematurely, after his mother was startled by news of the approach of the Spanish Armada. Educated at Magdalen Hall, Oxford, he translated some of Francis Bacon's essays into Latin, was mathematics tutor to the Prince of Wales, and met Galileo and Descartes on a tour of the Continent. He believed that the basis of all knowledge was sensation, and that our reactions are always aimed at self-preservation. From this he concluded that man was basically selfish and therefore needed an absolutist government to enforce law and order. This found him no supporters in the church, and unfortunately led the Royalists to believe he supported Cromwell. He also believed that man could be diverted from vice by poetry and he was a master of irony, not least in his work *Leviathan*, in which he compared the papacy to the kingdom of the fairies. A central feature of his philosophy was that the life of man is 'solitary, poore, nasty, brutish and short'.

Early trials of the sleeping policeman, as a traffic-calming measure exposed a few basic design flaws.

HISTORIC WORDS

Writing his *Britannia* in the glory days of Elizabeth I, William Camden, the antiquary and historian, saw no reason to be coy. His country was, as everyone knew, 'the most famous island without comparison of the whole world'. And what made it especially enviable, he also knew, was its weather. Britain was, he rejoiced, 'seated as well for aires as soile in a right fruitfull and mild place. The aire so kinde and temperate that not only the Summers be not excessive hot by reason of continual gentle winds that abate their heat...but the winters are also passing mild.' It was this sweet fertility, Camden thought, that had made Britain so irresistible to the ancients. In *Happie Britaine*, according to the Roman writer known as the panegyrist of Constantine (whom the Elizabethans believed had been born there), 'the forests were without savage beasts and the ground voyd of noisome serpents. Contrariwise an infinite multitude there is of tame cattle with udders strutting full of milke.' Thus blessed, the historian Tacitus conferred on Britain the best compliment that could occur to any Roman: that it was *pretium victoriae* (worth the conquest).

Simon Schama,
A History of Britain

Britons who just kept on going:

The Right Reverend Thomas Wilson served as a bishop for 57 years until he died in office in 1755.

Sir Robert Walpole served as Prime Minister for 20 years and 326 days, working into his sixty-sixth year.

Queen Victoria was still on the throne when she died at the age of 81. Her reign lasted 63 years, seven months and three days.

Winston Churchill wrote *A History of the English-speaking Peoples,* aged 82.

William Ewart Gladstone became Prime Minister for the fourth time at the age of 82 and remained PM for two years.

W Somerset Maugham wrote *Points of View,* aged 84.

David Lloyd George, former Prime Minister, remarried, aged 87.

Harry Phillips from Shropshire served as a chorister at his local church from 1893 (aged eight) to 1983 (aged 90).

George Bernard Shaw wrote *Far-fetched Fables,* aged 93.

Lord Maenan made his maiden speech in the House of Lords in 1948, at 94 years and 123 days.

HABEAS CORPUS

In the late eighteenth century, Scotsman John Aitken had one ambition: to make a name for himself. Having failed to distinguish himself at work, in the army or in America, where he lived for a few years, he set out instead to help America win their war for independence. He planned to do this by the simple expedient of setting fire to all of Britain's shipyards. He managed to set only a few small fires in Portsmouth and Bristol, but it was enough to rattle the authorities. Assuming the arsonist was American, Parliament rushed through a bill that allowed American privateers to be held indefinitely without charges. Their reason was 'it may be inconvenient in many such cases to proceed forthwith to the trial of such criminals, and at the same time of evil example to suffer them to go at large.' This was called the American High Treason Bill, and it caused a number of suspects to be imprisoned without trial in both American and British prisons. However, Aitken was not one of them; when he was eventually caught, he was quickly tried and hanged. The Bill was allowed to lapse when the war was over and Britain's inhabitants regained their right not to be held without trial.

The Battle of Waterloo is a work of art with tension and drama with its unceasing change from hope to fear and back again, change which suddenly dissolves into a moment of extreme catastrophe, a model tragedy because the fate of Europe was determined within this individual fate.
Stefan Zweig, Austrian writer

WILLIAM COBBETT AND THE POTATO PROTEST

William Cobbett (1763-1835) was a self-educated farmer's son who became the most famous journalist of his generation, thanks to his refusal to be silenced. After serving as a soldier, he obtained his discharge and retired first to France, then to America, where he wrote his first work *The Life and Adventures of Peter Porcupine*, a dangerously pro-British work that did not endear him to the Americans. He returned to England in 1800 and soon shifted from an anti-Radical position to that of Radical. He wrote extensively and forcefully on a wide variety of subjects, and was in favour of such things as universal suffrage and turnips, but very much against Shakespeare, tea and paper money. He was once imprisoned for publishing an attack on flogging in the army, but continued to publish from his prison cell. When an MP referred to his paper as 'two-penny trash', Cobbett obligingly renamed his publication *Cobbett's Two-penny Trash*, which considerably improved his sales figures.

He had strong views, which he recorded in exceptional detail, and had a particular hatred for potatoes, which he thought reduced man to the status of a pig. 'I would see all these labourers hanged and be hanged with them myself rather than see them live upon potatoes,' he thundered. 'Beware of the blasphemous cant of sleek-headed Methodist thieves that would persuade you to live upon potatoes.' He even suggested that the people overthrow the government in order to be free of this wretched vegetable, and protestors did indeed march on Parliament, bearing potatoes stuck on sticks. Cobbett also published a series of essays called *Cobbett's Rural Rides* in which he admired the 'real' countryside and took exception to anything he considered ornamental or fake, such as pruned trees. Despite his prison record and incitement to riot, he was twice elected to Parliament before he died in 1835, just 10 years before the terrible potato famines in Ireland.

MADE IN BRITAIN

When	Who	Invented what
1711	John Shore	Tuning fork
1712	Thomas Newcomen	First piston-operated steam engine, used to drive water pumps
1740	James Lind	Treatment for scurvy
1757	John Campbell	Sextant
1759	John Harrison	First chronometer accurate enough to allow precise measurement of longitude at sea, for which he was awarded a £20,000 prize by the Board of Longitude
1778	James Watt	Duplicating machine
1780	William Addis	Toothbrush with handle and bristles
1782	H Sidgier	First washing machine, a wooden cage turned by a handle
1789	Andrew Meikle	Threshing machine to separate grains from husks
1795	Joseph Bramah	Hydraulic press
1796	Edward Jenner	Smallpox vaccination

HISTORIC WORDS

Muv taught English history from a large illustrated book called *Our Island Story*, with a beautiful picture of Queen Victoria as its frontispiece. 'See, England and all our Empire possessions are a lovely pink on the map,' she explained. 'Germany is a hideous mud-coloured brown.' The illustrations, the text, and Muv's interpretative comments created a series of vivid scenes: Queen Boadicea, fearlessly riding at the head of her army... the poor little Princes in the Tower... Charlemagne, claimed by Grandfather as our ancestor... hateful, drab Cromwell... Charles I, Martyred King... the heroic Empire Builders, bravely quelling the black hordes of Africa for the glory of England... the wicked Indians of the Black Hole of Calcutta... the Americans, who had been expelled from the Empire for causing trouble, and who no longer had the right to be a pretty pink on the map... the Filthy Huns, who killed Uncle Clem in the war... the Russian Bolshies, who shot down the Czar's dogs in cold blood (and, as a matter of fact, the little Czarevitch and Czarevnas, only their fate didn't seem quite so sad as that of the poor innocent dogs)... the good so good, and the bad so bad; history as taught by Muv was on the whole very clear to me.

Jessica Mitford,
Hons and Rebels

132 *House number on Long Acre, London, occupied by John Logie Baird, inventor of the television*

*The lamps are going out all over Europe;
we shall not see them lit again in our lifetime.*
Edward Grey, First Viscount Grey of Falloden, in 1914

LOST VILLAGES

It is estimated that there are more than 3,000 'lost villages' in England. The most common reason for their disappearance was the Black Death, when the plague wiped out entire rural populations, and no one wanted to go back for fear of infection. Many were destroyed by war, while in the monastic expansions of the early medieval period, many villages were removed in to make way for a new monastery. In the eighteenth century many super-rich landowners did much the same thing, when looking for the perfect site for their new country estate.

However, many other villages disappeared under more drastic circumstances. Hallsands in Devon was destroyed in 1917 when all but 30 of its cottages were swept away by the sea, while a village under the cliffs at St Ishmael's in Carmarthenshire has been buried under the sand since it disappeared during the great storms of 1606.

Many villages were lost as a result of the building of new reservoirs, among them Derwent and Ashopton in Derbyshire, Mardale in Cumbria, and West End in Yorkshire. Local folklore has it that when the water level is low, the old church tower of West End can still be seen, and its ghostly bell rings out as a lament for the lost village. The same is said of Sutton Bingham in Dorset and Capel Celyn in Wales, as well as other villages 'lost' to the sea, including Shipden in Norfolk and Mabelthorpe in Lincolnshire.

Several villages were not so much lost as stolen, such as Tottington in Norfolk, Imber in Wiltshire and Tyneham in the same county. In all cases, the villages were commandeered by the military during wartime for live-firing practice, with the promise that they would be returned to their owners after the war. They never were.

But there is one village that is more than happy to stay lost – the village of Lost in Upper Donside, Scotland. Aberdeenshire Council was determined to rename the village Lost Farm, after the village's road sign was stolen four times in five years by souvenir-hunting tourists. But in October 2004 the villagers clubbed together to pay for a new sign, which is welded to an eight-foot pole which is in turn embedded in concrete.

KINGDOM OF ENGLAND

House of Wessex

Alfred the Great	871-899
Edward (the Elder)	899-924
Athelstan	924-939
Edmund I	939-946
Eadred	946-955
Eadwig/Edwy	955-959
Edgar the Peaceful	959-975
Edward the Martyr	975-978
Aethelred the Unready	978-1013 and 1014-16
(Swein Forkbeard	1013-1014)
Edmund II Ironside	1016

House of Denmark

Canute the Dane	1016-1035
Harthacnut	1035-37 and 1040-42
Harold I, Harefoot*	1037-1040
Edward the Confessor	1042-1066
Harold II	1066

House of Normandy

William I	1066-1087
William II	1087-1100
Henry I	1100-1135

House of Blois

Stephen	1135-1154**

House of Anjou

Henry II	1154-1189
Richard I	1189-1199
John	1199-1216

House of Plantagenet

Henry III	1216-1272
Edward I	1272-1307
Edward II	1307-1327
Edward III	1327-1377
Richard II	1377-1399

House of Lancaster

Henry IV	1399-1413

Henry V	1413-1422
Henry VI	1422-61 and 1470-71

House of York

Edward IV	1461-70 and 1471-83
Edward V	1483
Richard III	1483-1485

House of Tudor

Henry VII (Tudor)	1485-1509
Henry VIII	1509-1547
Edward VI	1547-1553

House of Suffolk

Jane	1553

House of Tudor

Mary I	1553-1558
Elizabeth I	1558-1603

House of Stuart

James I	1603-1625
Charles I	1625-1649

Commonwealth and Protectorate

Oliver Cromwell, Lord Protector	1653-1658
Richard Cromwell, Lord Protector	1658-1659

House of Stuart

Charles II	1660-1685
James II	1685-1688

House of Orange

William III and Mary II (Mary died 1694)	1689-1702

House of Stuart

Anne	1702-1714

134 *Number of representatives in the House of Lords who voted in favour of female suffrage in 1917, with 71 votes against*

KINGDOM OF GREAT BRITAIN
(After the Act of Union between England and Scotland in 1707)

House of Hanover (Regent from 1811)		House of Saxe-Coburg-Gotha (Windsor from 1917)	
George I	1714-1727	Edward VII	1901-1910
George II	1727-1760	George V	1910-1936
George III	1760-1820	Edward VIII	1936
George IV	1820-1830	George VI	1936-1952
William IV	1830-1837	Elizabeth II	1952-present
Victoria	1837-1901		

*Harold was regent from 1035, but seized the throne for himself in 1037.

**In 1141, Stephen was briefly deposed by Matilda, who was eclared queen and 'reigned' for eight months, but was never crowned.

HISTORIC WORDS

15 January 1912

It is wonderful to think that two long marches would land us at the Pole. We left our depot today with nine days' provisions, so that it ought to be a certain thing now, and the only appalling possibility the sight of the Norwegian flag forestalling ours. Little Bowers continues his indefatigable efforts to get good sights, and it is wonderful how he works them up in his sleeping-bag in our congested tent. (Minimum for night −27.5°.) Only 27 miles from the Pole. We ought to do it now.

16 January 1912

Camp 68. Height 9,760. T. −23.5°. The worst has happened, or nearly the worst. We marched well in the morning and covered 7 1/2 miles. Noon sight showed us in Lat. 89° 42'S., and we started off in high spirits in the afternoon, feeling that tomorrow would see us at our destination. About the second hour of the march Bowers' sharp eyes detected what he thought was a cairn; he was uneasy about it, but argued that it must be a sastrugus. Half an hour later he detected a black speck ahead. Soon we knew that this could not be a natural snow feature. We marched on, found that it was a black flag tied to a sledge bearer; near by the remains of a camp; sledge tracks and ski tracks going and coming and the clear trace of dogs; paws – many dogs. This told us the whole story. The Norwegians have forestalled us and are first at the Pole. It is a terrible disappointment, and I am very sorry for my loyal companions. Many thoughts come and much discussion have we had. Tomorrow we must march on to the Pole and then hasten home with all the speed we can compass. All the day-dreams must go; it will be a wearisome return.

From the diary of Captain Robert Falcon Scott, Antarctic explorer

*The leader writer in a great Northern daily said on the morning
after King Edward died that if he had not been a king he would
have been the best type of sporting publican.*
James Agate, British film and drama critic

BRITAIN'S FIRST UNIVERSITIES

University	Founded
Oxford	1249
Cambridge	1284
St Andrew's	1411
Glasgow	1451
Aberdeen	1495
Edinburgh	1583
UMIST	1824
Durham	1832
London	1836
Manchester	1851

WITCHES, PROPHETS AND MYSTIC MEN

William Lilly

When London burned down in the Great Fire of 1666, the authorities cast around for someone to blame. Among others, they arrested one William Lilly, the most famous astrologer in England, who was also known as the English Merlin. In 1665, Lilly had published a pamphlet showing Gemini, the astrological sign for London, falling headfirst into a fire. Somehow it was concluded that his prediction had caused the fire – or perhaps he had started it himself to raise his profile. The authorities had reason to believe his prophesies; his advice had been sought by Charles I and Cromwell in turn, and in 1644, in a pamphlet called *The Prophecy of the White King*, he foresaw that the royal army would be defeated, and a 'white king' would bring misery to the country, and would die soon after. Many thought this to be Charles I, who had been crowned in white rather than the traditional purple. When the royal army was defeated at the Battle of Marston Moor and the King was later tried and executed, the government turned to Lilly for his sage advice. However, by the time Charles II was restored to the throne, Lilly had fallen out of favour. He was tried for starting the Great Fire, but managed to convince the jury that he was just the messenger and was acquitted. He promptly left the city and kept the rest of his prophecies to himself until he died in 1681.

Pints of milk needed to make one 17-pound Stilton cheese, first made in Stilton in the eighteenth century

OLD PICTURE, NEW CAPTION

*Centuries before Saddam Hussein employs look-alikes as
a protection against his enemies, Richard III has the same idea.*

THE FIRST KNIGHTS OF THE GARTER

- King Edward III
- Edward (his son), Prince
  of Wales, the Black Prince
- Henry, Duke of Lancaster
- Thomas, Earl of Warwick
- Piers de Creilly, Captal
  de la Bouch
- Ralph, Earl of Stafford
- William, Earl of Salisbury
- Roger, Earl of March
- Sir John Lisle
- Sir Bartholomew Burghersh
- Sir John Beauchamp
- Sir John Mohun
- Sir Hugh Courtenay
- Sir Thomas Holland
- Sir John Grey
- Sir Richard Fitz-Simon
- Sir Miles Stapleton
- Sir Thomas Wale
- Sir Hugh Wrottesley
- Sir Nele Loring
- Sir John Chandos
- Sir James Audley
- Sir Otho Holland
- Sir Henry Eam
- Sir Sanchet Daubrichcourt
- Sir Walter Paveley

One of the radioactive substances (caesium 137) that was released into the
atmosphere after a fire at the Windscale nuclear reactor in 1957 137

ELEVEN INTERESTING FACTS ABOUT YORK

- The Roman name for York – Eboracum – means 'the place of the yew trees'.

- York is one of the two oldest surviving dukedoms (the other is Gloucester). The title Duke of York was created for Edmund of Langley by his nephew, Richard II.

- York is exactly halfway between London and Edinburgh: about 165 miles each way.

- York Minster is the largest gothic cathedral in northern Europe and took 252 years to build.

- York contains 19 medieval churches.

- The Hansom Cab pub is named after Joseph Hansom, who designed the Patent Safety Cab in 1834.

- The film *Elizabeth*, about the life of Elizabeth I, was the first film to be allowed to use the interior of York Minster as a location.

- York is the most haunted city in Europe, and is home to a whole host of ghosts including the spirits of a troop of Roman soldiers, which were last seen in 1953.

- York has the longest and best-preserved town walls in England, 3.4km long. They include 45 towers.

- Guy Fawkes was born and educated in York; St Peter's School, which he attended, does not burn a guy on Bonfire Night.

- The Yorkie chocolate bar is made in York (as is the KitKat). York has long been a centre for confectionery, and both Rowntree and Terry's of York began there.

- It is still legal to shoot a Scotsman with a bow and arrow in York, but only within the city walls, and only after dark.

EARLY TRIBAL KINGS

Some of Britain's earliest known or legendary tribal leaders

Beli Mawr, c.100BC, King of Silures and High King,
possibly the father of Lud and Caswallon

Lud/Llud, c.70-60BC, King of Silures, High King, founder of London

Caswallon, c.60-48BC, King of Cateuvellauni and High King

Imanuentus, c.55BC, King of Trinovantes, murdered by Caswallon

Mancubracius, c54-30BC, King of the Trinovantes,
possibly the grandfather of Boudicca

Cingetorix, c55BC, one of the tribal leaders of the Cantii in Kent, led
an attack on Caesar's ships off Kentish coast

Commius, c50-20BC, from Belgic tribe of Atrebates, forced out of the
country, returned as Caesar's agent but later rebelled against him

WHO WAS THE REAL ST GEORGE?

It has always been a puzzle that St George, patron saint of England, was not in fact an Englishman. So who was he? It was long thought that he was a Greek Prince of Cappadocia, but this has been disputed by modern historians. It is known that he was a soldier and that he was tortured and beheaded for his Christian beliefs, supposedly at Lydda in Palestine about 304AD. But that is almost all that is known about him. It would seem that, rather in the manner of King Arthur (who was also not a true Briton), a legend has been created from a few vital details – Christian, soldier, hero – and has been embellished until it fits our requirements of a patriotic hero.

George was officially designated the patron saint of England by Pope Benedict IV (900-903), and from that point Britain accepted him as one of their own. English churches were dedicated to him before the Norman Conquest, notably Doncaster in 1061. The Crusades of the thirteenth century then added to George's popularity, as his image was used as a symbol of English Christianity and of heroism. William of Malmesbury, the great medieval chronicler, said that St George and St Demetrius, 'the martyr knights', were 'seen' assisting the Franks at the battle of Antioch in 1098. It is also generally accepted that the 'arms of St George' (a red cross on a white shield) were introduced about the time of Richard the Lionheart (Richard I), himself a dedicated Crusader. In 1284, the armorial seal of Lyme Regis contained a ship flying a plain flag, bearing a cross, and the large red St George's cross on a white ground is still the 'White Ensign' of the Royal Navy. It is also, of course, one of the elements of the Union Flag. In the fourteenth century, St George's arms were officially adopted by English soldiers and sailors. Finally, King Edward III made St George the principal patron of the Order of the Garter, which the King founded around 1348, which established once and for all the iconic status of this mysterious Christian knight.

STILL LIFE

An oft-repeated story about James, Duke of Monmouth, is that a portrait of his dead body hangs in the National Portrait Gallery, painted after he was executed for attempting to claim the throne. The story claims that his head and body were reattached and his portrait was quickly completed before he was reburied. Sadly, the gallery dismisses the story as nonsense, and says that the portrait in question is of an unknown man. But the painting still has a ghoulish secret; it was not uncommon to paint a corpse to preserve the sitter for posterity, and the mysterious portrait is almost certainly that of a dead man.

The song that has been unofficially adopted as the national anthem of Scotland (mainly by followers of the Scottish rugby team) was written to commemorate the defeat of King Edward II by Robert Bruce at Bannockburn in 1314, when the Scottish King's forces overpowered the much larger English forces.

Flower of Scotland

O Flower of Scotland,
When will we see your like again
That fought and died for
Your wee bit hill and glen.
And stood against him,
Proud Edward's army,
And sent him homeward
Tae think again.

The hills are bare now,
And autumn leaves lie thick and still
O'er land that is lost now,
Which those so dearly held
That stood against him,
Proud Edward's army
And sent him homeward
Tae think again.

Those days are past now
And in the past they must remain
But we can still rise now
And be the nation again!
That stood against him
Proud Edward's army
And sent him homeward
Tae think again.

O Flower of Scotland,
When will we see your like again
That fought and died for
Your wee bit hill and glen.
And stood against him,
Proud Edward's army,
And sent him homeward
Tae think again.

Who the first inhabitants of Britain were, whether natives or immigrants, remains obscure; one must remember we are dealing with barbarians.
Tacitus, Roman historian

TEN DAYS THAT TIME FORGOT

In any historical account of Britain, it can be guaranteed that from 3 to 13 September 1752, absolutely nothing happened – because the days never existed.

At the time Britain was still using the Julian calendar, a system introduced by Julius Caesar in 45BC. The calendar that had preceded it was a complicated affair that required a group of pontiffs to decide when days should be added or subtracted to keep the dates in harmony with the seasons. The system was open to bribery and error, so Caesar abolished it and replaced it with a year that measured 365.25 days. This meant that a year was 365 days long, but every fourth year was 366 days long. He also inserted extra months in the first year of his calendar, which made the year last 445 days, and caused it to be known as the 'last year of confusion'. The first year of this calendar began on 1 January, 46 years before the birth of Christ.

However, this system created an error of one day every 128 years, which, over time, would result in a complete dislocation of dates from their seasons, which became apparent only as the centuries passed. Finally, a sixteenth century physician from Naples called Aloysius Lilius came up with the Gregorian calendar (named after the Pope). In this system, a year was 365.2425 days long, and required 97 leap years every 400 years to remain stable. Lilius's calendar was anchored by the occurrence of the vernal equinox, which was supposed to take place on 21 March. Because it was by now 1582 and the error of one-in-128-days had been accumulating over the years, the vernal equinox was occurring 10 days early. So it was decided to remove 10 days from the year to realign the date.

The Gregorian calendar came into use in 1582, after a papal bill was issued to that effect by Pope Gregory XIII. All countries adopting the calendar promptly removed 10 days from their year, five to 14 October. Most of the Catholic countries fell into line, but many others – including Britain – did not. Britain in fact held out until 1752, by which time it had to remove 11 days from the calendar to keep in step. It was decided that 11 days would be lost from September, so what should have been 3 September was called 14 September. The days of 3 to 13 September 1752 were lost for ever.

Bertie begins to realise that 'Trust me, baby, I'm the Prince of Wales' has finally lost its effectiveness as a chat-up line.

HISTORIC WORDS

By the wrath of God, Queen of England, Duchess of Normandy, unhappy mother, pitied by no one, the wife of two kings, I have arrived at this miserable old age which plunges me into ignominy. I was also the mother of two kings. The Young King and the Count of Brittany lie in dust and their unhappy mother is doomed to be incessantly tortured by their memory. Two sons remain but they exist to add to my miseries. King Richard is in irons; his brother John ravages the kingdom with fire and sword. I know not which side to take. If I leave, I abandon the kingdom of my son torn by civil war, the country bereft of wise council and consolation. If I stay I may never see the dearly beloved face of my son again.

A letter from Eleanor of Aquitaine to the pope
Despite her tone, it could be said that Eleanor had brought her misfortunes upon herself. Eleanor, wife of Henry II, bore her husband eight children, but encouraged her sons to conspire against their father, which they did – Henry, Richard and John all fought the English king. John was Henry's youngest and favourite son, and on learning of John's role in this treachery, the King died, it is said, of heartbreak. Richard inherited the throne, but John was quick to seize it when Richard was imprisoned abroad while on crusade. Eleanor lived to be 82, conspiring with her sons to the last.

Sir Francis Bacon (1561-1626)

Educated at Trinity College, Cambridge from the age of 12 or 13, Francis Bacon became a barrister in 1582 and soon after was elected to Parliament. Although not always in favour with Elizabeth I, and often in debt, he prospered, although it was James I who made him a knight, solicitor-general, attorney-general, lord keeper and lord chancellor. However, Bacon's career ended when he pleaded guilty to taking bribes, and was effectively cast out of society. He turned to writing and produced a considerable body of work during his life, including *The Advancement of Learning*, in which he classified all the different branches of knowledge, which proved to be a model of secular thought much referred to by later writers. He wrote several more substantial volumes on science and natural history and planned more on philosophy and the intellect, which were never completed. He was a scientist at heart, and believed that it was man's duty to unlock nature's mysteries in order to gain true control over their lives. In a fiercely religious age, he was at heart an empiricist. He wrote a history of Henry VII, which sought to explain, rather than merely chronicle the King's life in the usual manner, and addressed other subjects including legal principles in *Maxims of the Law* and a series of renowned *Essays*. He died of pneumonia while experimenting with the possibility of freezing food.

STRANGE CUSTOMS

Coracle Regatta

Every August in Cilgerran, Cardiganshire, the Coracle Regatta takes place on the River Teifi, where the waters cascade through a spectacular gorge. Fishermen have used coracles to fish in this country for centuries, and the races are a tribute to the enduring usefulness of this peculiar craft. The village of Cilgerran is at the top of a wooded gorge, and the regatta takes place in the shadow of the old Cilgerran castle that overlooks the river. Various races are held, including single-handed, ladies only and 'foreign' coracles – that is, not of the very specific River Teifi type. Members of the countrywide Coracle Society are made welcome, although the Teifi coracles try fiercely not to be out-run on their own territory. The coracles are made from a willow frame bound with hazel wood, covered with calico cotton and waterproofed with hot pitch and linseed oil. They weigh about 30lbs and can be carried on the back like a turtle shell. The older coracles were much heavier, giving rise to the Welsh saying 'Llwyth gwr, ei gorwg' – 'A man's load is his coracle'.

Vanloads of royal furniture removed from Brighton Pavilion after the building
was sold in 1849

ENGLISH PLACE-NAMES

Place-names in England largely divide into **habitative**, such as 'high homestead' or 'long farm', and **topographical** like 'green hill' and 'clear stream'. There is also a smaller group of names that refers to the **settling-place** of a particular tribe, usually shown by an –ing ending, such as Hastings, meaning 'Haesta's people'. Below are some common elements of familiar place names around the country:

brough	fortified place (also burgh, bury, borough, burgh, bury)
by	farmstead, village
cester	city, town, walled camp (also chester, caster)
fleet	estuary, stream
font	spring (also hunt)
gate	way, road, street (also yate, yatt, yet)
ham	manor, homestead
hay	hedge, fence, enclosed land
hope	dry land in fen, small valley, blind valley (also hop, op, up)
hythe	port, haven (also hive, hithe, eth)
kirk	church
lac	stream, watercourse (also lake, lock, lack)
linch	bank, ridge (also lynch, ling, linge)
mede	meadow (also made, med, meadow)
minster	monastery, church
over	bank, ridge, hill
peth	path, track (also path)
rick	strip of land, narrow road, also ridge
rith	stream (also reth, red)
scough	wood (also skew, scoe)
shaw	copse, grove, small wood
shire	division of the people, division of the kingdom
stowe	holy place, place of assembly (also stoe)
thwaite	meadow, clearing
toft	site of a house, homestead, enclosure
wold	woodland, forest, high forest, open upland (also wald, walt, wal, wauld, old, would)
wark	work, fortification
wath	ford (also with, worth)

QUOTE UNQUOTE

How is the Empire?
The last words of King George V, according to prime minister
Stanley Baldwin, although the King's physician claimed that
George's last words were, in fact, 'God damn you'

144 *Number of people, mostly children, killed in the Aberfan coal tip disaster in 1966*

Britain's worst military disaster took place in January 1842 in Afghanistan. The ruler of Afghanistan, the Amir Dost Mohammed, was so anti-British that Lord Auckland was determined to depose him and substitute Shah Suja, an Afghan noble. Suja was friendly towards the UK and was being kept in India on an allowance for just this purpose. In August 1839, a force of British and Indian troops, grandly called the 'Army of the Indus', invaded Afghanistan and occupied Kandahar, Ghazni and Kabul.

The occupation lasted for 18 months, but after a revolt and the murder of two political agents, it was decided to evacuate the garrisons in the capital. Seven hundred and fifty British and 2,250 Indian troops with between 10,000 and 12,000 camp followers left Kabul on 6 January 1842. The weather was abysmal, the ground was covered in snow and the temperature was below freezing. Waiting for them in the mountain passes were the Afghan Ghilzais with their extra-long-barrelled rifles called Jezails. Trained almost from birth, they were reckoned to be the finest marksmen in the world and they had a devastating effect on the long, slow column. The soldiers with their smooth bore muskets stood little chance against them.

It is popularly believed that there was only one survivor of the massacre, a military surgeon called Dr William Bryden, who reached Jellalabad, a fort garrisoned by the Thirteenth, First-Somerset Light Infantry and some native troops. The rest were totally annihilated by the Afghans or succumbed to the appalling weather. In fact, six other men survived, with a few wives and children, who had been held as hostages in Kabul and were later released. In addition, a few Indian sepoys straggled in later.

MONARCH MNEMONIC

How to remember your kings and queens
Willie, Willie, Harry, Stee
Harry, Dick, John, Harry Three
One, two, three Neds, Richard Two
Harries Four Five Six – then who?
Edwards Four, Five, Dick the Bad
Harries twain and Ned the Lad
Mary, Bessie, James the Vain
Charlie, Charlie, James again
William and Mary, Anna Gloria
Four Georges, William and Victoria
Edward, George, the same again
Elizabeth the Second, and long may she reign!

The fate of some famous remains:

Anne Boleyn's heart

After she was beheaded on the orders of Henry VIII, Anne's heart was stolen and hidden in a church near Thetford in Suffolk. It was reburied under the church organ in 1836.

Charles I's vertebra

In 1813, the coffin of Charles I was opened and an autopsy performed by royal surgeon Sir Henry Halford. He took a fancy to the king's fourth cervical vertebra and took it home to use at dinner parties as a salt holder. The vertebra was later returned at Queen Victoria's request.

Sir Walter Raleigh's head

After his beheading, Raleigh's wife Elizabeth had his head embalmed and kept it by her side in a leather bag for the rest of her life. Their son Carew kept the head safe until his death in 1666, when it was buried with him and the rest of his father's body. The son, and Raleigh's head, were eventually reburied in West Horsley, Surrey.

Shelley's heart

When romantic poet Percy Bysshe Shelley drowned in Italy in 1822, his body was cremated on the beach. One of his friends, Edward Trelawney, noticed that the heart was not burned, and pulled it from the flames. He gave it to Shelley's friend Leigh Hunt, who gave it to Mary, Shelley's wife. She wrapped it in silk and carried it everywhere, until their son Percy also died, and she buried the heart with him.

WITCHES, PROPHETS AND MYSTIC MEN

Elizabeth Barton

Elizabeth Barton (1506-1534) was a servant-girl who became a national celebrity after a serious illness plunged her into a trance. Through the haze of fever she began to foresee the future, and was quickly taken under the wing of the church, who considered her prophecies to be messages from heaven. Soon she was being used as propaganda for the Catholic Church and became something of a celebrity. When King Henry VIII tried to divorce his first wife, Catherine, it was the perfect opportunity for the Church to use Elizabeth to condemn his action, as if in a message directly from God. 'If this king does not desist in this impious action, he will die within seven months and his daughter, Mary, will rule in his stead,' Elizabeth proclaimed. Henry took little notice, divorced Catherine and married Anne Boleyn. The country held its breath. When the King failed to expire after seven months, public opinion turned against Elizabeth Barton, and the King swiftly had her arrested and hanged for treason.

THE LIFE OF BYRON

Few of Britain's most famous scoundrels have pursued self-destruction with quite the gusto of George, Lord Byron. Famous for his romantic poetry, Byron himself could not have been less romantic. Born to an unfaithful and profligate father who killed himself, Byron's life started badly and ran rapidly downhill. At Harrow he formed relationships with younger boys, and at university in Cambridge he frequented prostitutes, fell in love with a choirboy and began an affair with a girl called Caroline, whom he liked to dress as a boy. On a tour of Europe he spent much of his time with prostitutes or young men before returning to make his maiden speech in the House of Lords in 1812. The publication of *Childe Harold's Pilgrimage* – the tale of a hedonistic young man – made him famous, and he took full advantage of the female attention that followed.

He had a stormy relationship with Lady Caroline Lamb, who coined the phrase 'mad, bad and dangerous to know', but left her to start an affair with his half-sister, who became pregnant. He included the theme of incest in his verse novel *The Bride of Abydos*. He married an heiress, Annabella Milbanke, with whom he committed such unnatural acts that her horrified parents took her back. He was often drunk, bad-tempered and broke, and when London society began to turn its back on him, he left the country after a last fling with Claire Clairmont, who became pregnant. Ensconced in Venice he kept his house stocked with prostitutes and lovers, including the landlord's wife and a countess named Teresa. But when Teresa left her husband, Byron promptly left her and fled to Greece, where he died of a fever. He was just 37.

CELTIC TREASURES

Some of Britain's earliest Celtic treasures in the British Museum

Witham Shield: bronze
• Third century BC
River Witham, Lincolnshire

Aylesford bucket: wood and bronze • First century BC
Aylesford, Kent

Battersea shield: bronze
• Second to forth century BC
River Thames, London

Two-horned helmet: bronze
• First or second century BC
River Thames, London

Scabbard ornament:
bronze • 200BC
Mill Hill, Deal, Kent

Mirrors: bronze
• First century BC
Desborough, Northamptonshire

*Number in thousands of people living in South Africa in 1904 who were born 147
in England or Wales*

The first King of Scotland is often said to be Alpin, but many prefer to give that title to his son Kenneth MacAlpin. He became King of the Scots in 834 on the death of his father, but in 840 he also became King of the Picts, and so was the first king of all Scotland

House of Alpin

Kenneth I MacAlpin	834-58
Donald I	860-863
Constantine II	863-877
Aedh	877-878
Eocha	878-889
Donald II	889-900
Constantine III	900-942
Malcolm I	942-954
Indulf	954-962
Duff	962-967
Colin	967-971
Kenneth II	971-995
Constantine IV	995-997
Kenneth III	997-1005
Malcolm II	1005-1034

House of Atholl

Duncan I	1034-1040
Macbeth	1040-1057
Lulach	1057-1058
Malcolm III Canmore	1058-1093
Donald III Bane	1093-1094
Duncan II	1094
Donald III Bane	1094-1097
Edgar	1098-1107
Alexander I	1107-1124
David I The Saint	1124-1153

Malcolm IV The Maiden	1153-1165
William I The Lion	1165-1214
Alexander II	1214-1249
Alexander III	1249-1286
Margaret The Maid of Norway	1286-1290

House of Balliol

John Balliol	1292-1296

House of Bruce

Robert I (Bruce)	1306-1329
David II	1329-1371

House of Balliol

Edward Balliol	1332/1333-1346

House of Stewart

Robert II	1371-1390
Robert III	1390-1406
James I	1406-1437
James II	1437-1460
James III	1460-1488
James IV	1488-1513
James V	1513-1542
Mary, Queen of Scots	1542-1567
James VI*	1567-1625

In 1603, on the death of Elizabeth I, James VI became James I of England, after which the kingdoms were ruled by one monarch.

QUOTE, UNQUOTE

We call up to seven men 'thieves'; from seven to thirty-five 'a band'; above that is an army.
Alleged words of Ine, King of the West Saxons (688-726)

Nursery rhymes and children's songs often commemorate famous historic people and events. Here are three popular interpretations:

Old King Cole – There was an Old King Coel in Britain in the late fourth and early fifth century, who ruled the northern Britons. However, he was not the only Coel around at this time, which has given rise to some confusion about his being the Lord of Colchester, which was another Coel altogether. As for the 'fiddlers three', there is no record that Coel was musical, nor that he was even a merry old soul.

The Grand Old Duke of York – this is most likely to have been Richard, Duke of York, who was killed in the Wars of the Roses. At the Battle of Wakefield in 1460, Richard marched his troops up to Sandal Castle, which was at the top of a hill, and at some point marched down again, abandoning his safe haven to make a direct attack. It failed, and he was killed.

Three Blind Mice – Queen Mary, known as Bloody Mary, owned vast estates with her husband, Philip of Spain, hence the reference to a farmer's wife. The three blind mice were three Protestant noblemen convicted of conspiring against the Queen, who was a staunch Catholic. She in fact had them burned at the stake rather than dismembered.

THE DAY CRIPPEN'S HEAD FELL OFF

On 7 June 1931, Britain's largest recorded earthquake struck at Dogger Bank, measuring 6.0 on the Richter scale. The tremors were felt all over Britain and as far away as France, Belgium, Germany, the Netherlands and Norway. The greatest damage was reported down the east coast, including the town of Filey, where a church spire was completely rotated. Minor damage occurred as far south as Suffolk, and a factory roof collapsed in Staines. The *Daily Mail*, whose headline read: 'People thrown from their beds' reported that the country shook from Edinburgh to Bournemouth. It also reported the unexpected casualty of Dr Crippen's waxwork in Madame Tussaud's in London. The head of his effigy was shaken off and landed on the foot of Arthur Devereux, the Kensal Rise murderer, who was displayed next to him. As the *Mail* reported: 'Dr Crippen was left standing in his replica of the Old Bailey dock with half a moustache on one shoulder and his spectacles dangling from the other.' Several other waxworks were damaged, including that of tennis player Helen Wills Moody, who lost her right arm. The only real person reported dead was a woman in Hull who died of a heart attack, allegedly brought on by the shock.

Number in thousands of people living in British North America (Canada) in 149 1891 who were born in Ireland

THE BATTLE THAT NEVER WAS

On 24 February 1797, a small French force of three ships of war and a lugger anchored in a small roadstead near Fishguard and proceed to disembark troops. Lord Cawdor, the local militia officer, in his report later said that, on hearing the news, he proceeded to the spot with a detachment of the Cardigan Militia and 'all the provincial forces he could collect'. However, he failed to mention in his report the Castle Martin Yeomanry, who got there before him. But Lord Milford, the Lord-Lieutenant of the county, also wrote a report, which said that 'before the troops arrived, many thousands of the peasantry turned out, armed with pikes and scythes, to attack the enemy'. Legend has it that the magnificence of the yeomanry's uniforms convinced the French that they were part of a much larger army, more of whom appeared on the hills overlooking the bay. The 'troops' on the hills were, in fact, a large number of local Welsh ladies, dressed in their tall black hats and red cloaks, marching up and down in a fearsome manner. But the French were deceived, and promptly surrendered.

The yeomanry eventually did get the credit for their prompt turnout and were belatedly awarded their Battle Honour in 1853, the only Battle Honour to be won in Britain.

HISTORIC WORDS

My loving people, we have been persuaded by some that are careful of our safety to take heed how we commit ourselves to armed multitudes for fear of treachery, but I assure you I do not desire to live to distrust my faithful and loving people. Let tyrants fear; I have always so behaved myself under God, I have placed my chiefest strength and safeguard in the loyal hearts and goodwill of my subjects. And therefore I am come amongst you, as you see, at this time not for my recreation and disport, but being resolved in the midst and heat of battle to live and die amongst you all. To lay down for God, my kingdom and for my people, my honour and my blood even in the dust. I know I have the body of a weak and feeble woman, but I have the heart and stomach of a King and a King of England too and think it foul scorn that Parma or Spain or any Prince of Europe should dare to invade the borders of my realm; to which, rather than any dishonour shall grow by me, I myself will take up arms, I myself will be your General, Judge and Rewarder of every one of your virtues in the field. I know already for your forwardness you have deserved rewards and crowns; and we do assure you, on the word of a Prince, they shall be duly paid you.

Elizabeth I to her troops as they awaited the Spanish Armada

DURING THE COMPILATION OF THIS BOOK, THE COMPANION TEAM...

Reconstructed the Battle of Medway, at which the Britons fought bravely, but the Romans still won

Painted their faces with woad for the staff party

Attempted to name all the British monarchs in order, but kept leaving out King Stephen

Tried to invent something as clever as the traffic light, the tin opener or the concept of parliamentary democracy

Staged a Peasants' Revolt to call for extra bread in the canteen

Set off bravely for the 'North Pole', which would have been an historic expedition had it not been the name of a pub just up the road

Recreated the first glider flight in miniature, using lollysticks, paper, glue and a very long corridor

Failed to agree on whether King Richard I was a Good Man or a Bad King

Wondered how they ever passed their history 'O' Level without knowing the difference between a vassal and a villein

Please note that although every effort has been made to ensure accuracy in this book, the above statistics may be the result of aged and ancient minds.

History, especially British history with its succession of thrilling illuminations, should be, as all her most accomplished narrators have promised, not just instruction but pleasure.

Simon Schama

The answers. As if you needed them.

P16.   The Channel Islands – but he lost the rest of the duchy of Normandy, which at that time belonged to England.

P24.   Elvis Presley, aka 'The King' (two hours at Prestwick Airport in Scotland in 1960).

P31.   A way of walking affected by ladies at the court of Queen Alexandra, wife of Edward VII, to make the Queen's own slight limp less noticeable.

P41.   The seven hills of Rome: Capitoline, Quirinal, Viminal, Esquiline, Caelian, Aventine, Palatine.

P53.   This is the combined total of the years reigned by all eight King Henrys, the longest total for any single name.

P60.   Colonel Robert Baden-Powell, so named by the various African tribes whom he met on his travels.

P68.   Hugh Gaitskell imposed charges on dental (and ophthalmic) treatment to contribute to the costs of the Korean War. The remainder of treatments on the recently introduced NHS remained free.

P78.   King Richard III, killed while fighting the forces of Henry Tudor (later Henry VII) at the Battle of Bosworth in 1485.

P83.   His father, Adrian Bell, compiled the first cryptic crossword, in *The Times*, published on 1 February 1930.

P96.   There are 16 drams in an ounce.

P102. They were sixteenth century double strength beers, which the London authorities tried to ban.

P107. Cooking; they are all crops grown in medieval England.

P117. A jamboree – the *Oxford English Dictionary* now defines this word as 'a collection of Boy Scouts' after the first mass rally at Olympia in London in 1920.

P125. Both are buried in Winchester Cathedral.

NOTES, THOUGHTS AND JOTTINGS

Number of years after Lord Palmerston faced a motion for impeachment that certain MPs suggested the same be done to Tony Blair

FURTHER READING

The Assassin's Cloak, Edited by Irene and Alan Taylor

Book of Dignities, J Haydn

The Book of Lists, David Wallechinsky,
Irving Wallace, Amy Wallace

The Book of Prophecies, Jonathan Dee

The British Monarchy in Colour, John Brooke-Little

Chronicle of the World, Edited by Derrik Mercer

Cassell's Companion to Twentieth Century Britain, Pat Thane

The Customs and Ceremonies of Britain, Charles Kightly

A Dictionary of Twentieth Century World Biography,
Edited by Asa Briggs

Flushed with Pride: The Story of Thomas Crapper,
Wallace Reyburn

Food and Feast in Medieval England, PW Hammond

A History of Britain, Volume I, Simon Schama

The Mammoth Book of British Kings and Queens, Mike Ashley

The Oxford Companion to the English Language,
Edited by Tom McArthur

The Oxford Companion to English Literature,
Edited by Margaret Drabble

The Penguin Illustrated History of Britain and Ireland,
Barry Cunliffe

A People's History of Britain, Rebecca Fraser

Rogues, Villains and Eccentrics, William Donaldson

The Royal Line of Succession, Pitkin Books

The Royal Palaces, Philip Howard

The Shell Book of Firsts, Patrick Robertson

A Social History of England, Asa Briggs

Steinberg's Dictionary of British History,
SH Steinberg and IH Evans

The Top Ten of Everything 2004, Russell Ash

The Year 1000, Danny Danziger and Robert Lacey

History... is, indeed, little more than the register of the crimes, follies, and misfortunes of mankind.

Edward Gibbon

ACKNOWLEDGEMENTS

We gratefully acknowledge permission to reprint extracts of copyright material in this book from the following authors, publishers and executors:

Europe: A History of Britain by Norman Davies, first published by Oxford University Press, reproduced by permission of Oxford University Press.

Journalism: Truth or Dare? by Hargreaves, Ian (2003) (pp.37-38). By permission of Oxford University Press.

Rules of Desire by Cate Haste reproduced by permission of Faith Evans Associates.

Hons and Rebels by Jessica Mitford reprinted by permission of The Estate of Jessica Mitford.

Why I Write (Copyright © George Orwell 1953) reproduced by permission of AM Heath & Co. Ltd on behalf of Bill Hamilton as the Literary Executor of the Estate of the Late Sonia Bronwell Orwell and Martin Secker & Warburg Ltd.
Excerpt from *Why I Write* in *Such, Such Were the Joys* by George Orwell, copyright 1953 by Sonia Bronwell Orwell and renewed in 1981 by Mrs George K Perutz, Mrs Miriam Gross, and Dr Michael Dickson, Executors of the Estate of Sonia Bronwell Orwell, reprinted by permission of Harcourt, Inc.

Extract from *A History of Britain: Volume 1* by Simon Schama reproduced with the permission of BBC Worldwide Limited. Copyright © Simon Schama 2000.

INDEX

FILL YOUR BOOKSHELF AND YOUR MIND

The Birdwatcher's Companion Twitchers, birders and ornithologists are all catered for in this unique book. ISBN 1-86105-833-0

The Cook's Companion Foie gras or fry-ups, this tasty compilation is an essential ingredient in any kitchen. ISBN 1-86105-772-5

The Countryside Companion From milking stools to crofters tools, this book opens the lid on the rural scene. ISBN 1-86105-918-3

The Fishing Companion This fascinating catch of fishy facts offers a whole new angle on angling. ISBN 1-86105-919-1

The Gardener's Companion For anyone who has ever gone in search of flowers, beauty and inspiration. ISBN 1-86105-771-7

The Golfer's Companion From plus fours to six irons, here's where to find the heaven and hell of golf. ISBN 1-86105-834-9

The History of Britain Companion All the oddities, quirks, origins and stories that make our country what it is today. ISBN 1-86105-914-0

The Ideas Companion The stories behind the trademarks, inventions, and brands that we come across every day. ISBN 1-86105-835-7

The Legal Companion From lawmakers to lawbreakers, find out all the quirks and stories behind the legal world. ISBN 1-86105-838-1

The Literary Companion Literary fact and fiction from Rebecca East to Vita Sackville-West. ISBN 1-86105-798-9

The London Companion Explore the history and mystery of the most exciting capital city in the world. ISBN 1-86105-799-7

The Moviegoer's Companion Movies, actors, cinemas and salty popcorn in all their glamorous glory. ISBN 1-86105-797-0

The Politics Companion Great leaders and greater liars of international politics gather round the hustings. ISBN 1-86105-796-2

The Sailing Companion Starboards, stinkpots, raggie and sterns – here's where to find out more. ISBN 1-86105-839-X

The Shakespeare Companion A long, hard look at the man behind the moustache and his plethora of works. ISBN 1-86105-913-2

The Traveller's Companion For anyone who's ever stared at a plane and spent the day dreaming of faraway lands. ISBN 1-86105-773-3

The Walker's Companion Ever laced a sturdy boot and stepped out in search of stimulation? This book is for you. ISBN 1-86105-825-X

The Wildlife Companion Animal amazements and botanical beauties abound in this book of natural need-to-knows. ISBN 1-86105-770-9